ideals

Mexican COOKBOOK

by Barbara Grunes

Introduction

The cuisine of Mexico is a blend of five thousand years of the various cultures which have inhabited the land. The agrarian Mayans and Aztecs provided the basis of the cuisine with their corn, beans, squash, and peppers. Further enhanced by the olives, wheat, rice, beef, pork and wine brought by the Spanish conquistadors, Mexican cooking also incorporates the refined cooking techniques of the French who briefly ruled the country. This colorful cuisine is a combination of regional specialties, such as *Ceviche* from Acapulco, *Sopa de Lima* from the Yucatan and *Turkey with Nogada Sauce* from Puebla—all complemented by the great variety of chilies.

This book dispels the myth that all Mexican food is hot and spicy, since much of the cuisine is a subtle blend of flavors contained in sauces, rice dishes, desserts and festive breads. And there is always the vibrant color of the many fruits and vegetables which make these dishes festive as well as delicious.

Most of the recipes in this book require no special ingredients, and substitutions for hard-to-find items are listed in the recipe or glossary.

So plan a Mexican fiesta and enjoy it right in your own dining room. Olé!

ISBN 0-8249-3000-2

Published by Ideals Publishing Corporation
11315 Watertown Plank Road
Milwaukee, Wisconsin 53226

Contents

Acknowledgment

Sincere thanks to Senoras
Anna Brener of Mexico City and
Carmen Vasquez for their help
in preparing this book.

Edited and designed by Julie Hogan

Let's Talk Chilies

Chilies are an integral part of the Mexican cuisine. They are available fresh or dried, mild or hot.

The hotness of chilies varies from region to region and even among the same kind of chilies. Before adding any chili to the dish you are preparing, carefully taste the chili with the tip of your tongue. If the chili is too hot, reduce the amount called for in the recipe, substituting sweet green pepper for the remainder.

The hot quality of the chili comes from a substance in the veins of the pepper called *capsaicin.* This substance can cause hours of discomfort if it comes into contact with sensitive areas, such as the eyes. It is important, therefore, to wash your hands with soap and water immediately after handling chilies. People with very sensitive skin should wear rubber gloves.

If a particular chili is unavailable, look for it canned. Some chilies can be substituted for others, but the differences between chilies are subtle. Experience will teach you which chilies may be substituted when a particular variety is unavailable. If all else fails, substitute ground red pepper or hot pepper sauce.

Fresh Chilies

Jalapeno Small, shiny, dark green pepper. One of the best known of the chilies. Often available in American supermarkets fresh, canned or pickled; also in canned sauces. They are about two and one-half inches long and very hot. There are no real substitutes, but if *jalapeno* chilies cannot be obtained, use *serrano* chilies.

Serrano Smaller than the *jalapeno* chili, but also very hot. They are about one inch long and one-half inch wide. Use judiciously. Available fresh or canned, sometimes pickled. As with other fresh chilies, they are toasted, peeled, seeded and deveined before using.

Poblano *Poblano* chilies are mild to mildly hot. They can be made less hot by removing seeds and veins. They vary in size, but resemble a dark green bell pepper. Substitute bell peppers or *anaheim* chilies if *poblano* chilies are unavailable.

Bell pepper Bell peppers are deep green, red when fully ripened. A very sweet and mild pepper.

Guero Pale yellow in color, with a waxy sheen. They vary in size to about four inches. Not readily available.

Anaheim or **California** Readily available fresh in supermarkets. They are green and about six inches long and one to two inches wide. They are a sweet, mild pepper. Also available canned.

Banana peppers Tapered, yellow peppers commonly found in most supermarkets. Mildly flavored, they are often stuffed.

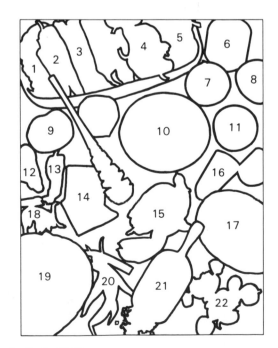

What Is It?

The photo opposite contains many of the chilies described on pages 2 and 4 and ingredients listed in the glossary on page 5.

1. Serrano chilies
2. Banana peppers
3. Jalapeno chilies
4. Dried ancho chilies
5. Poblano chilies
6. Nopalitos
7. Pickled serrano chilies
8. Pickled jalapeno chilies
9. Jicama
10. Tomatillos
11. Canned chipotle chilies
12. Dried mulato chilies
13. Dried pasilla chilies
14. Mexican chocolates
15. Tamarind pods
16. Piloncillo
17. Dried jamaica
18. Dried serrano chilies
19. Nopales
20. Dried New Mexico pasilla chilies
21. Achiote
22. Dried cascabel or guajillo chilies

Dried Chilies

Ancho The *ancho* chili is the dried form of the *poblano* chili. It is a mild to mildly hot chili that imparts full-bodied flavor. The *ancho* is brownish-red in color and about four to five inches long. *Anchos* are available in Mexican grocery stores, but if unavailable, substitute up to two teaspoonsful chili powder.

Cascabel Small, round chilies with a smooth skin and brownish-red color. *Cascabels* have a mild, slightly nutty taste.

Cayenne Very hot chili. Available in supermarkets. Use sparingly.

Chipotle A smoked *jalapeno*. These are very hot chilies. They are about 2½ inches long and bright red in color. They have a smoky taste. Also available canned.

Mulato The *mulato* chili is similar to the *ancho* chili, but is almost brown in color. It has a tapered end and a more pungent flavor.

Pasilla Long, slim and somewhat darker in color than the *ancho* chili. *Pasilla* chilies are about five to six inches long and approximately one inch wide. They are a little less rich and slightly more spicy than the *ancho* chili. *Pasillas* can be substituted for *ancho* chilies.

Pequin A small red-hot chili available in most supermarkets. May be crushed. Substitute crushed red peppers or *cayenne* chilies if *pequin* chilies are unavailable.

Preparation of Fresh Chilies

Remove the skin of fresh chilies before using. To do so, place the chilies on a skewer. Using a pot holder, hold the skewer over a gas flame. Rotate the chilies as they begin to blister and become charred. Place chilies in the middle of a tea towel and fold the towel over them or place them in a plastic bag and close it. Allow chilies to steam for fifteen minutes. The skin loosens and will be easy to peel. Remove the peel, seeds and veins.

Another way to remove the skin is to place the chilies on a broiler pan about three inches beneath the flame. Turn the chilies as they begin to blister. Proceed as instructed above.

Preparation of Dried Chilies

To reconstitute dried chilies, toast them gently in an ungreased skillet to soften them. Then place chilies in a saucepan, cover with water and boil for four minutes, or until they are soft. Drain, remove stem and seeds. Puree in a blender or food processor with just enough liquid to make a paste. Save the cooking water to use in soup or thin a sauce.

Preparation of Canned Chilies

Canned chilies should be rinsed in cold water before proceeding. They are then seeded and chopped as necessary.

Where to Find Ingredients

Chicago Area

Casa Cardenas
324 South Halstead
Chicago, Illinois 60606

Casa del Pueblo
1810 Blue Island
Chicago, Illinois 60608

Casa Esteiro
2719 West Division
Chicago, Illinois 60622

New York Area

Casa Moneo
210 West 14th Street
New York, NY 10014
(212) 929-1644
Mail orders,
Cooking equipment

Trinacaria Importing Co.
415 Third Avenue
New York, NY 10014
(212) LE2-5567

Boston Area

Garcia Superette
367 Center Avenue
Jamaica Plain
Boston, MA 01230

Los Angeles

El Mercado
First Avenue and Lorena
Los Angeles, CA 90063

Milwaukee

Rubens Quality Foods
1135 W. Mitchell
Milwaukee, WI 53204

Elrey Mexican Foods
1000 South 16th St.
Milwaukee, WI 53204

Denver

El Molino Foods, Inc.
1078 Santa Fe Drive
Denver, CO 80204

San Antonio

Frank Pizzini
202 Produce Row
San Antonio, TX 78207
Mail orders

San Francisco

La Palma
2884 24th Street
San Francisco, CA 94110
(415) 648-5500

Sante Fe

Theo. Roybal Store
Rear 212-216 Galistero St.
Santa Fe, NM 87501
Mail Orders,
Cooking Equipment

Seattle

Mexican Grocery
1914 Pike Place
Seattle, WA 98101

Glossary

Achiote (ah-chee-OH-tay) Seed from the annatto tree used to flavor food and color it a delicate shade of yellow. Dried seed is cooked in heated oil until the color changes.

Burrito (boohr-EE-toh) A large flour *tortilla* wrapped around a filling.

Chayote (chie-OH-tay) A pear-shaped, light green vegetable, member of the cucumber family.

Chocolate What we think of as chocolate is somewhat different in the Mexican cuisine. Its origins trace back to a time when it was so highly valued that it was used as money. Mexican chocolate is a mixture of chocolate, cinnamon and sugar. Often sold in tablet form or in blocks. A *molinillo* (wooden beater) is used to beat hot chocolate until it is frothy. (See photo on page 3.)

Chorizo (chor-EE-so) A spicy pork sausage that can be very hot or mild. It is available in Mexican grocery stores and can also be made at home. Italian sausage can be substituted.

Cilantro (see-LAHN-tro) Fresh coriander. Available in Oriental markets. Also called Chinese parsley.

Enchilada (en-chee-LAH-dah) *Tortilla* that has been dipped in sauce, filled and rolled. It is then covered with a sauce and baked.

Epazote (ay-pah-ZOH-tay) An herb used for seasoning. It has a strong flavor, but is considered essential to flavor black beans.

Jamaica (ha-MIKE-ah) Dried red hibiscus flowers. They are soaked in water to make a drink for hot weather. Available at Mexican grocery stores.

Jicama (HEE-kih-mah) A white root vegetable, similar to the potato in texture. They are peeled, sliced or cubed and used in salads or sprinkled with chili powder and served as an appetizer.

Masa (MAH-sah) Dough made of *masa harina* and lard, used to make *tortillas.*

Masa harina (MAH-sah a-REE-nah) Flour made from ground corn. Used to make *masa.* Available in large supermarkets.

Mole (MOH-lay) Spicy sauce served with turkey or chicken. Made from a paste of chilies, chocolate and other ingredients. Available in specialty food stores.

Nopales (noh-PAH-lays) or **Nopalitos** (noh-pah-LEE-tohs) The edible pads of the *Opuntia* cactus. When choosing fresh *nopales,* select the thinnest and smallest pads. To prepare, remove thorns, cut pads into small pieces and cook in boiling, salted water until tender. Drain and wash until all of the skin is removed. *Nopales* are also available canned.

Pepitas (peh-PEE-tahs) Unsalted, hulled pumpkin seeds. Often ground and used in sauces or the seeds can be served as an appetizer.

Piloncillo (pee-lon-SEE-yoh) Unrefined brown sugar molded into cones. To use, grate with a knife or a vegetable peeler. Can be purchased at Mexican groceries. Dark brown sugar can be substituted.

Plátanos (PLAH-tan-ohs) Plantain. A starchy fruit resembling bananas. Purchase when black and soft to the touch. Available at Mexican groceries year round. Bananas may be substituted.

Taco (TAH-ko) May be either a soft *tortilla* or one that has been crisply fried in hot lard or oil. They may be folded in half or rolled around a filling. Eaten as a snack in Mexico.

Tamales (ta-MAH-lees) Made of *masa* dough, filled and wrapped in fresh or dried corn husks and steamed. They are generally eaten as a meal by themselves. The sweet *tamales* are eaten as a dessert. *Tamales* with no filling are served as a bread with a meal.

Tamarindo (TAH-ma-rin-do) Flavorful pod of the tamarind tree. It is used to make a refreshing beverage. Available in Mexican groceries.

Tomatillos (toh-mah-TEE-yohs) A tart fruit with a paper-like husk. Always cooked before using. They add a lovely green color and piquant flavor to sauces. Store in refrigerator wrapped in paper. Available, canned or fresh, at Mexican groceries.

Tortillas (tor-TEE-yahs) The staff of life of the ancient Mexicans. *Tortillas* are a flat bread made of corn or wheat flour, either rolled by hand or flattened with a press. Available ready-made in most supermarkets.

Tostadas (tos-TAH-das) *Tortillas* fried until almost crisp and used to make something like an open-faced sandwich.

Antojitos y Bebidas
(Appetizers and Beverages)

Empanaditas *Cocktail-Size Turnovers*

- 4 tablespoons vegetable oil
- 1 medium onion, chopped
- 2 cups Refried Beans (Recipe on page 43) or
  1 15-ounce can refried beans
- 2 packages empanadita pastry or 2 pie crusts cut
  into 20 circles with a cookie cutter or glass
- 1 extra large egg, lightly beaten
- 3 cups vegetable oil

Heat oil in a ten-inch skillet. Add onion and sauté for two minutes, stirring occasionally. Stir in beans and cook for two minutes; cool. Use ready-made empanadita pastry circles or prepare pie crust. Place a tablespoon of refried beans on each pastry circle. Fold in half, seal with egg and twist edges. Heat oil to 375° in a large saucepan. Deep fry four empanaditas at a time, until golden brown on each side. Drain on paper toweling. Serve warm with Mexican beer. Makes 20.

Cold Chopped Eggplant

- 2 medium eggplants
- 3 tablespoons vegetable oil
- ½ teaspoon garlic powder
- 1 teaspoon dried onion flakes
- 1 large tomato, peeled, chopped
- 3 tablespoons chopped cilantro
- ¼ teaspoon salt
- 1 4-ounce can mild chilies, rinsed, seeded,
  chopped and drained

Choose eggplants that are firm, have glossy skins and rich color. Pierce eggplants with a fork. Place in a 400° oven for thirty-five minutes, or until tender. Remove pulp from eggplants and chop; place in a large mixing bowl. Add oil, garlic powder and onion flakes; mix well. Add remaining ingredients; mix lightly. Cover with plastic wrap; chill one hour before serving. Serve with tortillas and olives. Makes 3 cups.

Nachos

- 4 7-inch flour tortillas
- 2 cups vegetable oil
- ½ teaspoon garlic salt
- 8 ounces Monterey Jack cheese, grated
- 1 cup sliced black olives

Cut each tortilla into six wedges with scissors. Heat oil to 375° in a skillet. Fry six tortilla chips at a time until golden brown on both sides, about one minute. Remove with a slotted spoon. Drain on paper toweling. Place tortilla chips on a baking sheet. Preheat oven to 400°. Sprinkle tortilla chips with garlic salt, cheese and olives. Bake until the cheese melts. Serve hot. Makes 24.

Pickled Shrimp

- 1 pound small fresh shrimp, cooked, shelled
  and deveined
  Juice of 4 limes
  Juice of 2 lemons
- 1 large red onion, thinly sliced
- 1 cup green olives
- 3 tablespoons wine vinegar
- 1 tablespoon olive oil
- ½ teaspoon red pepper flakes
- ½ teaspoon salt
- ¼ teaspoon white pepper
- 2 tablespoons chopped parsley

Combine all ingredients in a glass bowl. Cover with plastic wrap. Refrigerate for six hours, turning every two hours. Garnish with parsley. Makes 6 to 8 servings.

Fried Squash Blossoms

- 12 squash blossoms (Raise your own, or can be
  purchased at a Mexican grocery store in
  early summer.)
- 4 ounces grated Monterey Jack cheese
- 1 jumbo egg, separated
- ½ cup all-purpose flour
- ½ cup vegetable oil

Remove stems from blossoms. Fill centers with cheese. Seal blossoms with a toothpick. Beat egg white until soft peaks form. Dust blossoms with flour. Beat egg yolk until light-colored. Dip blossoms in egg yolk and then in egg white. In a small saucepan, heat oil to 375°. Fry blossoms two at a time until golden brown on both sides. Remove with a slotted spoon; drain on paper toweling. Remove toothpicks and serve. Makes 6 servings.

Cocktail Meatballs

¾ pound ground beef
½ pound ground pork
1 extra large egg, lightly beaten
½ cup milk
¼ cup light cream
5 green onions, chopped
½ teaspoon chili powder
½ teaspoon ground cumin
½ teaspoon salt
1½ cups bread crumbs
½ teaspoon oregano
5 tablespoons vegetable oil
2 cups Veracruz Sauce (Recipe on page 52)

Combine all ingredients, except bread crumbs, oregano, oil and sauce in a large mixing bowl. Make small, cocktail-size meatballs. Combine bread crumbs and oregano; mix lightly. Heat oil in a twelve-inch skillet. Roll meatballs in bread crumbs. Fry meatballs until browned on all sides and completely cooked. Place in a chafing dish or bowl; cover with heated Veracruz Sauce. Serve warm. Makes about 35 to 40 meatballs.

Fried Plantain Chips

3 large ripe plantains
3 tablespoons butter
3 tablespoons vegetable oil
Salt

Slice the tips off the plantains. Cut plantains in thirds; peel off skin with a knife. Slice plantains on the diagonal, one-quarter-inch thick. Heat butter and oil in a twelve-inch skillet. Fry on both sides until golden brown. Drain on paper toweling. Sprinkle with salt. Serve hot, as a vegetable or an appetizer. Makes 6 servings.

Guacamole

1 large avocado, peeled and pit removed
2 tablespoons lemon juice or lime juice
8 ounces cream cheese, at room temperature
½ teaspoon salt
½ teaspoon Tabasco sauce

Place avocado in a large mixing bowl and mash. Add remaining ingredients; mix well. Place in a covered container and refrigerate until ready to use. Serve with fried tortilla chips, enchiladas or vegetables. Makes 2½ cups.

Bean Dip

1 15-ounce can refried beans
2 cups sour cream
½ teaspoon garlic powder
½ teaspoon ground cumin

Combine all ingredients in a small bowl. Correct seasoning, if necessary. Cover and refrigerate until ready to serve. Serve with fried tortilla chips. Makes 3½ cups.

Chocolate Mexicano *Mexican Chocolate*

3 ounces Mexican chocolate
4 cups milk
4 2-inch cinnamon sticks, optional

Combine all ingredients in a heavy two-quart saucepan. Simmer until the chocolate has melted; beat all ingredients with a whisk or a *molinillo* (a Mexican wooden beater used to make the chocolate drink frothy. See photo on page 3). Serve in a mug with a cinnamon stick. Makes 4 drinks.

Note: To substitute for Mexican chocolate, use 4-ounces semisweet chocolate, ¾ teaspoon cinnamon and ¼ teaspoon vanilla.

Margarita *Tequila Cocktail*

1 lime wedge
1 tablespoon coarse salt
1 ounce tequila
½ ounce lime juice
½ ounce Triple Sec

Rub the rim of a cocktail glass with lime wedge. Pour the salt into a saucer. Dip the glass into the salt. Shake tequila, lime juice and Triple Sec with ice. Strain into the prepared glass. Makes 1 drink.

Refreshing Tamarind Drink

½ pound tamarind pods
3 quarts water
½ cup pineapple juice
2 cups granulated sugar

Clean tamarinds by removing peel and washing. Place all ingredients in a large glass bowl. Cover with aluminum foil and refrigerate for two days. Strain through cheesecloth. Correct seasoning. Serve chilled. Makes 3 quarts.

Sangrita

This spicy drink is served with tequila.

1 small onion, minced
  Juice of 2 limes
½ teaspoon cayenne pepper
4 cups canned tomato juice
1 cup orange juice
  Tequila to serve 12
½ cup salt
12 lime wedges

Combine all ingredients, except salt and lime wedges, in a blender or food processor for four seconds. Pour into a large, chilled pitcher filled with ice cubes. To serve, strain into tall cocktail glasses. Place salt in a small bowl. Wet edges of whiskey glasses; dip into salt to make a rim of salt. Serve Sangrita with tequila and a wedge of lime. Makes 12 servings.

Mango Ice

1½ cups water
 1 cup granulated sugar
 4 tablespoons lime juice
 2 cups mango pulp
 1 cup milk

Combine water and sugar in a medium-size saucepan. Bring to a boil and cook for five minutes, without stirring. Cool to room temperature. Combine lime juice, mango pulp and milk. Add to sugar syrup. Place mixture in freezer trays. Freeze for three hours. Place in a mixing bowl and beat until soft and smooth. Return to freezer trays and place in freezer about six hours, or until solid. May also be made with an ice cream maker following manufacturer's directions. Serve as ice cream. Makes 6 to 8 servings.

Sangria *Red Wine and Fruit Punch*

1 fifth red wine, such as Burgundy
1 cup superfine sugar
⅓ cup brandy
  Juice of 1 large orange
3 cups bottled carbonated water, chilled
2 oranges
2 lemons
2 limes

Combine wine, sugar, brandy and orange juice in a large, chilled pitcher. Refrigerate for one hour. When ready to serve, add carbonated water; mix well. Slice oranges, lemons and limes. Float fruit slices in pitcher. Serve chilled in punch glasses or in cocktail glasses with ice cubes. Makes 12 cups.

Tequila Sunrise

  Ice cubes
1½ ounces tequila
½ cup orange juice
1 tablespoon grenadine
1 slice orange

Place ice cubes in a cocktail glass. Add tequila and orange juice. Pour grenadine into glass; stir. Place orange slice on side of glass. Serve immediately. Makes 1 drink.

Tequila Sour

1½ ounces tequila
⅛ teaspoon bitters
½ ounce lime juice
2 teaspoons superfine sugar
  Crushed ice
1 slice lime

Chill a whiskey-sour glass. Combine tequila, bitters, lime juice and sugar with ice. Shake well and strain into prepared glass. Garnish with lime slice. Serve immediately. Makes 1 drink.

Iced Coffee

½ teaspoon vanilla
¼ teaspoon ground cloves
¼ teaspoon cinnamon
3 cups cold coffee
  Crushed ice
8 tablespoons light cream

Place vanilla, cloves and cinnamon in a medium-size mixing bowl. Pour coffee over spices; let stand for fifteen minutes. Fill four tall glasses with crushed ice. Strain coffee over ice. Add two tablespoons cream to each glass. Makes 4 servings.

Pineapple Atole

1½ cups crushed pineapple, drained
¼ cup masa harina
¼ teaspoon cinnamon
3 cups milk
½ cup firmly packed brown sugar
½ teaspoon vanilla

Combine pineapple, masa harina, cinnamon and one cup of the milk in a medium-size saucepan. Cook over low heat, stirring often, until mixture begins to thicken. Remove from heat. Add remaining milk, sugar and vanilla. Return to heat and bring to a boil over moderate heat, stirring constantly. Serve hot in a coffee mug. Makes 6 servings.

Gazpacho

Chilled tomato and vegetable soup.

- 5 cups tomato juice
- 1 large cucumber, peeled, seeded and sliced
- 1 medium onion, minced
- 1 large green pepper, chopped
- 2 tablespoons olive oil
- 2 tablespoons red wine vinegar
- ½ teaspoon salt
- ¼ teaspoon Worcestershire sauce
- ¼ teaspoon Tabasco sauce
- 1 large cucumber, thinly sliced for garnish
- 1 large tomato, peeled, seeded and chopped

Combine first nine ingredients, in a large bowl. Cover with plastic wrap and refrigerate for two hours before serving. When ready to serve, pour gazpacho into soup bowls. Garnish with cucumber slices and chopped tomato. Serve cold. Makes 8 servings.

Cold Avocado Cream Soup

- 2 medium avocados
- 2 tablespoons lemon juice
- 2 extra large egg yolks
- ¼ teaspoon salt
- ¾ cup granulated sugar
- 1 quart chicken stock
- 2 cups heavy cream

Peel and mash avocados. In a large, chilled mixing bowl, combine avocados, lemon juice, egg yolks, salt, sugar and chicken stock. Using a small, chilled bowl, beat cream until soft peaks form. Gently stir cream into soup. Cover and chill soup for two hours before serving. Makes 8 to 10 servings.

Cold Tomato Soup

- 1½ tablespoons olive oil
- 2 cloves garlic, minced
- 1 small onion, chopped
- 1 4-ounce can mild green chilies, rinsed, seeded, drained and chopped
- 2 tablespoons all-purpose flour
- 1 35-ounce can tomatoes, mashed with liquid
- 3 cups chicken broth
- 1 chicken bouillon cube
- ¼ teaspoon salt
- ⅛ teaspoon pepper
- ¼ teaspoon ground cumin
- ½ teaspoon honey or 1 teaspoon sugar
- 1 cup sour cream

Heat oil in a five-quart stockpot over moderate heat. Add garlic, onion and chilies and cook for two minutes, or until onion is soft, stirring often. Stir flour into onion mixture. Add tomatoes, chicken broth, bouillon, salt, pepper, cumin and honey to onion mixture. Bring soup to a boil; reduce heat and simmer, covered, for twenty-five minutes, stirring once every five minutes. Remove from heat; cool. Remove to a large storage bowl; cover with plastic wrap. Refrigerate at least four hours before serving. Ladle soup into chilled bowls or mugs. Garnish each bowl of soup with a dollop of sour cream. Makes 8 servings.

Lentil Soup

- 4 slices bacon
- 2 cloves garlic, minced
- 1 large onion, chopped
- 2 large tomatoes, peeled, or 1 16-ounce can, including juice
- 1 large carrot, grated
- 3 large potatoes, quartered
- 1 pound lentils, washed
- 1 teaspoon salt
- ½ teaspoon pepper
- ½ teaspoon ground cumin
- 2 quarts water

Fry bacon in a Dutch oven. Drain bacon; reserve four tablespoons of the drippings. Heat drippings. Add garlic and onion and sauté for one minute, stirring occasionally. Dice bacon and add along with remaining ingredients. Cover and simmer for two hours, or until lentils are soft. Correct seasonings. Makes 6 servings.

Squash Soup

- 2 tablespoons vegetable oil
- 1 large onion, chopped
- 1 cup cooked ground pork
- 1 cup tomato sauce
- 3 medium tomatoes, peeled and chopped
- 2 large squash, thinly sliced
- 6 cups beef bouillon

Heat oil in a Dutch oven. Add onion and sauté for two minutes, or until onion is soft, stirring occasionally. Add remaining ingredients. Cover and simmer for forty minutes. Serve with warm tortillas. Makes 6 servings.

Chorizo and Noodles

1½ pounds chorizo or Italian sausage cut into
    1-inch pieces (Recipe on page 28)
  8 ounces thin noodles, broken in half
  1 35-ounce can tomatoes, chopped, reserve juice
  1 large onion, chopped
  ½ teaspoon salt
  1 4-ounce can hot chilies, rinsed, drained, seeded
    and chopped

Brown chorizo in a twelve-inch skillet, stirring occasionally. Remove chorizo; set aside. Leave three tablespoons drippings in the skillet; discard remaining drippings. Heat drippings. Add noodles and brown for two minutes, stirring constantly. Add chorizo, tomatoes, reserved juice, onion, salt and chilies. Cover and cook over moderate heat for ten to fifteen minutes, or until noodles are tender. Makes 4 to 5 servings.

Dry Chorizo Soup

  2 tablespoons vegetable oil
  1 large onion, chopped
1½ pounds chorizo or Italian sausage, cut into
    1-inch pieces (Recipe on page 28)
1¼ cups rice, washed and drained
2½ cups beef bouillon
  4 large tomatoes, peeled, seeded and chopped
  1 flour tortilla, crumbled

Heat oil in a twelve-inch skillet. Add onion and chorizo and sauté for four minutes, stirring occasionally. Drain drippings. Add rice and mix well. Add bouillon. Cook over moderate heat for fifteen minutes, stirring occasionally. Add tomatoes and crumbled tortilla and continue cooking until all ingredients are done. Serve hot in a deep bowl. Makes 4 to 5 servings.

Squash Blossom Soup

  4 tablespoons butter
  2 tablespoons vegetable oil
  2 cloves garlic, minced
  1 large onion, chopped
  6 ounces squash blossoms, chopped. (Raise your own
    or buy at a Mexican grocery store in early summer.)
  2 ears fresh corn or 2 cups canned corn
  8 beef bouillon cubes
  8 cups hot water
  ½ teaspoon salt
  ¼ teaspoon white pepper
  2 tablespoons chopped cilantro or parsley

Heat butter and oil in four-quart stockpot. Add garlic, onion and squash blossoms and sauté until soft, about two minutes, stirring occasionally. Cut kernels from cobs of corn; add to stockpot. Combine bouillon cubes and hot water in a large mixing bowl; stir to dissolve. Add bouillon, salt, pepper and cilantro to soup. Simmer, uncovered, for twenty minutes, or until the corn is tender. Serve hot in soup bowls. Makes 8 servings.

Black Bean Soup

  3 tablespoons bacon drippings
  2 cloves garlic, minced
  1 large onion, chopped
  1 pound black beans, washed and drained
  3 ribs celery, chopped
  4 cups water
  4 cups beef bouillon
  2 teaspoons salt
  ½ teaspoon pepper
    Beef bouillon or sherry
  2 cups sour cream

Heat bacon drippings in a five-quart stockpot. Add garlic and onion and sauté until soft, about two minutes, stirring occasionally. Add beans, celery, water and bouillon. Bring to a boil; reduce heat to a simmer, cover and cook for two hours. Stir in salt and pepper. Cover and simmer for one-half hour or until the beans are soft. Remove from heat and cool to room temperature. Strain beans, reserving liquid. Mash beans with a masher or in a food processor. Return beans to liquid and mix well. Thin soup to desired consistency with beef bouillon or sherry. Heat and serve with a dollop of sour cream. Makes 8 servings.

Sopa de Lima
Yucatan Chicken Soup with Lime

  3 tablespoons vegetable oil
  2 cloves garlic, minced
  ¼ cup chopped parsley
  1 cup chopped, cooked chicken
  8 cups chicken bouillon
    Juice of 1 large lime
    Lime slices for garnish

Heat oil in a Dutch oven. Add garlic and sauté for thirty seconds. Add remaining ingredients, except lime slices. Cover and simmer for twenty minutes. Serve hot with lime slices. Makes 6 to 8 servings.

Caldo de Pescado *Fish Soup*

- 5 tablespoons olive oil
- 3 large onions, chopped
- 2 16-ounce cans tomatoes, chopped, reserve juice
- ¼ cup white wine
- ¼ cup chopped parsley
- 4 bay leaves
- ½ teaspoon chili powder
- 2 quarts water
- ½ teaspoon salt
- 2½ pounds assorted firm-fleshed fish
- 6 slices toast, edges trimmed

Heat oil in a Dutch oven. Add onion and sauté for two minutes, stirring occasionally. Add tomatoes, wine, parsley, bay leaves and chili powder. Simmer for fifteen minutes. Remove bay leaves. Add water and salt. Bring soup to a boil. Add fish. Reduce heat, uncover and simmer for thirty minutes, or until the fish flakes easily. Place one slice of toast in each soup bowl. Ladle soup over toast and serve. Makes 6 servings.

Cream of Zucchini Soup

- ¾ pound zucchini
- 3 tablespoons butter
- 3 tablespoons all-purpose flour
- 5 cups milk
- ½ teaspoon salt
- ¼ teaspoon white pepper
- ¼ teaspoon nutmeg
- 1 cup sour cream, optional
- ¼ cup chopped pimiento, optional

Cut zucchini into one-inch chunks. In a saucepan, combine zucchini with enough water to cover and cook until tender. In a blender or food processor, combine zucchini and one cup of the cooking water; puree and set aside. Heat butter in a Dutch oven. Add flour; mix until flour is blended. Slowly stir in milk; add salt, pepper and nutmeg. Simmer until mixture begins to thicken. Add zucchini puree. Serve hot with a dollop of sour cream, sprinkled with pimiento. Makes 6 servings.

Caldo de Camarón *Shrimp Soup*

- ½ pound shrimp in shells
- 6 cups water
- 1 teaspoon allspice
- 1½ tablespoons vegetable oil
- 1 clove garlic
- 1 10½-ounce can condensed cream of tomato soup
  Pinch chili powder
  Salt and pepper to taste

Remove shells from shrimp. Place water in a medium-size saucepan. Place shells only in water. Add allspice. Bring to a boil. Boil for twenty minutes. Remove from heat and set aside. In another large saucepan, heat oil. Add garlic and sauté until garlic is golden. Discard garlic. Stir in tomato soup and shrimp. Strain water in which shells have been boiled. Add to soup-shrimp mixture. Bring to a boil and boil for twenty minutes. Stir in chili powder, salt and pepper. Makes 6 servings.

Garlic Soup

- 6 tablespoons olive oil
- 8 cloves garlic, mashed
- ¼ teaspoon cayenne
- 2 cups fresh bread cubes
- 2 quarts boiling water
- 4 beef bouillon cubes
- ½ teaspoon salt
- ½ teaspoon pepper
- 6 extra large eggs, lightly beaten

Heat oil in a Dutch oven. Add garlic and cayenne and sauté for thirty seconds. Remove garlic and set aside. Add bread cubes and fry until golden brown. Add water, bouillon, salt and pepper. Add garlic. Simmer, covered, for forty minutes. Slowly pour eggs into soup in a steady stream. Eggs will set in thirty seconds. Serve hot, with extra bread cubes. Makes 6 servings.

Sopa de Papas *Potato Soup*

- 3 large potatoes, peeled and quartered
- 1 large onion, chopped
  Water
- 1 teaspoon salt
- 2 slices bacon, fried, drained and crumbled, reserve drippings
- ½ teaspoon nutmeg
- ½ teaspoon white pepper
- 2 cups milk
- 1 cup light cream
- 3 tablespoons chopped parsley
- ¼ cup grated Cheddar cheese

Place potatoes in a two-quart saucepan. Add onion and cover with water. Sprinkle with salt. Cook potatoes until tender; drain and mash. Place mashed potatoes in a three-quart saucepan. Add bacon, two tablespoons drippings, nutmeg, pepper, milk and cream. Cook over low heat until soup is hot. Pour into individual bowls and garnish with parsley and Cheddar cheese. Makes 6 servings.

Ensaladas y Legumbres
(Salads and Vegetables)

Tossed Salad with Jicama

- 1 head iceberg lettuce, torn into bite-size pieces
- 3 large tomatoes, sliced
- 1 cup peeled, diced jicama
- 2 large, green bell peppers, seeded and sliced
- 1 large onion, sliced
- 4 slices bacon, fried, drained and crumbled, reserve drippings
- 1 teaspoon chili powder
- ½ teaspoon salt
- ⅓ cup red wine vinegar

Arrange lettuce in a large salad bowl. Arrange tomatoes, jicama, peppers and onion on lettuce. Sprinkle bacon on top. Combine chili powder, salt, vinegar and three tablespoons reserved bacon drippings; sprinkle over salad. Gently toss salad. Chill until ready to serve. Makes 6 servings.

Orange and Onion Salad

- 1 bunch romaine lettuce
- 6 medium oranges, peeled and sliced
- 2 medium red onions, sliced
- ½ cup sliced, pitted black olives
- ½ teaspoon salt
- ¼ teaspoon pepper
- 2 tablespoons minced basil
- 1 teaspoon minced mint
- 6 tablespoons olive oil
- 2 tablespoons wine vinegar
- 3 tablespoons minced parsley

Clean all lettuce and tear into pieces. Arrange lettuce on six salad plates. Place orange, onion and olives on lettuce. Sprinkle on salt and pepper. Mix basil, mint, olive oil and vinegar together in a bottle and drizzle over salad. Garnish with parsley. Makes 6 to 8 servings.

Steamed Plantain Salad

- 3 ripe plantains, peeled
  Whole lettuce leaves
- ¼ large head lettuce, sliced
- ½ cup chopped walnuts

Steam the plantains for ten minutes; slice in half lengthwise. Place lettuce leaves on six individual salad plates. Arrange sliced lettuce on top and place plantains on lettuce. Sprinkle walnuts over each salad. Serve with Vinegar and Oil Dressing. (Recipe on page 17.) Makes 6 servings.

Avocado Salad

- 2 cloves garlic, minced
- 4 tablespoons olive oil
- 4 tablespoons vegetable oil
- 1 tablespoon lemon juice
- 2 teaspoons tarragon vinegar
- ¼ teaspoon salt
- ⅛ teaspoon freshly ground black pepper
- 1 2-ounce can anchovy filets, drained and mashed
  Romaine lettuce, cut into bite-size pieces, optional
- 2 large ripe avocados, peeled and sliced
- 3 tablespoons lemon juice

Combine garlic, oils, lemon juice, vinegar, salt, pepper and mashed anchovies in a small mixing bowl. Arrange lettuce on a serving plate. Sprinkle avocado with lemon juice. Arrange avocado on lettuce. Sprinkle dressing over salad. Chill until ready to serve. Makes 6 to 8 servings.

Carrot Salad

- 5 large carrots, peeled and grated
  Juice of 1 large orange
- 3 tablespoons orange marmalade
- 3 tablespoons mayonnaise
- ⅛ teaspoon ginger
- ¼ teaspoon salt
- ½ cup raisins

Place carrots in a serving bowl. Combine orange juice, marmalade, mayonnaise, ginger and salt in a small mixing bowl. Toss carrots with dressing; chill. Sprinkle on raisins before serving. Makes 6 to 8 servings.

Pico de Gallo *Rooster's Bill with Jicama*

- 2 cups jicama, peeled, cut into ½-inch strips
- 1 11-ounce can mandarin oranges, drained, reserve juice
- ½ small head lettuce, thinly sliced
- 1 teaspoon ground ancho chili or chili powder
  Mandarin oranges for garnish, optional

In a large mixing bowl, combine jicama, mandarin oranges and one-third cup mandarin orange juice; toss lightly. Arrange lettuce on a serving plate. Place jicama mixture on lettuce; sprinkle chili powder on top. Garnish with mandarin oranges. Makes 4 servings.

Shrimp Salad in Avocado

1 pound frozen shrimp
2 tablespoons lime juice
¼ teaspoon salt
1 medium onion, thinly sliced
¼ cup olive oil
2 medium tomatoes, peeled and quartered
½ cup black olives
¼ teaspoon crushed red pepper
3 avocados, halved and seeded

Drop shrimp into boiling water. Cook only until the shrimp turn white. Drain shrimp; cool. In a medium mixing bowl combine lime juice, salt and onion; beat in the oil. Drizzle dressing over the shrimp; toss lightly. Combine tomatoes, olives and pepper; add to shrimp and toss lightly. Fill avocado shells with shrimp salad. Chill until ready to serve. Makes 6 servings.

Apple, Orange and Pineapple Salad

3 large oranges, peeled and chopped
4 large apples, peeled, cored and diced
1 8-ounce can pineapple chunks, drained
4 ribs celery, chopped
½ cup heavy cream, whipped
½ cup mayonnaise
½ small head lettuce, sliced
3 tablespoons brown sugar

In a large mixing bowl, combine oranges, apples, pineapple chunks and celery. Combine whipped cream and mayonnaise. Fold dressing into salad. Arrange lettuce on serving platter; place fruit on the lettuce and sprinkle brown sugar over the top. Cover loosely and chill until ready to serve. Makes 6 to 8 servings.

Ensalada de Jitomates *Tomato Salad*

½ medium head lettuce, sliced
6 large ripe tomatoes, thinly sliced
1 large avocado, seeded and sliced
1 cup sliced black olives
8 tablespoons vegetable oil
4 tablespoons wine vinegar
½ teaspoon salt
¼ teaspoon freshly ground pepper

Arrange sliced lettuce on eight individual salad plates. Place the tomatoes on the lettuce. Arrange the avocado and olives over the tomato. Combine vegetable oil, vinegar, salt and pepper; mix well. Drizzle over the salad. Chill until ready to serve. Makes 8 servings.

Ensalada de Nopalito *Cactus Salad*

1 19-ounce can nopalitos
1 large onion, thinly sliced
2 large tomatoes, peeled, seeded and chopped
¼ cup Vinegar and Oil Dressing (Recipe on page 17)
½ medium head lettuce, thinly sliced

Rinse nopalitos three times with cold water; drain. Place all vegetables, except lettuce, in a large mixing bowl. Sprinkle dressing over vegetables and toss lightly. Chill until ready to serve. Serve on sliced lettuce. Makes 5 to 6 servings.

Bell Pepper Salad

6 large red bell peppers
1 large onion, thinly sliced
3 tablespoons olive oil
3 tablespoons vegetable oil
3 tablespoons wine vinegar
2 tablespoons chopped parsley
½ teaspoon salt
¼ teaspoon ground black pepper

Hold each pepper over a gas flame until charred. Place peppers in a plastic bag or tea towel to steam for fifteen minutes. Remove the skins and seeds. Cut peppers into one-half inch strips; place in a serving bowl. Add remaining ingredients and toss lightly. Cover and refrigerate until ready to serve. Makes 6 to 8 servings.

Zucchini and Bean Salad

2 cups sliced, cooked zucchini
2 cups garbanzo beans
1 cup tarragon vinegar
¾ cup vegetable oil
2 tablespoons sugar
1 clove garlic, minced
1 teaspoon minced basil
⅛ teaspoon black pepper
 Lettuce leaves
¼ cup chopped green onion
2 medium tomatoes, cut in wedges

Arrange half of the zucchini in a baking dish. Place half of the beans on top of the zucchini. Combine vinegar, vegetable oil, sugar, garlic, basil and pepper in a covered jar; shake until well mixed. Pour half of the dressing over the vegetables. Arrange remaining zucchini and beans on top. Pour remaining dressing over all. Cover and refrigerate overnight. Before serving, drain dressing from vegetables, reserving one-quarter cup. Arrange zucchini and beans on lettuce leaves. Garnish with onion and tomato. Makes 6 to 8 servings.

Ensalada de Noche Buena

Christmas Eve Salad

- 2 small jicama, peeled and diced
- 3 slices fresh or canned pineapple, cubed
- 2 oranges, peeled and segmented
- ½ head iceberg lettuce, torn in bite-size pieces
- 2 bananas, peeled and sliced
  Unsalted peanuts
  Pomegranate seeds

Combine jicama, pineapple and oranges in a medium-size bowl. Place in refrigerator for one hour. Place lettuce on a serving platter. Add bananas to fruit mixture. Toss lightly. Arrange fruit on lettuce. Garnish with peanuts and pomegranate seeds. Makes 6 servings.

Ensalada de Coliflor *Cauliflower Salad*

- 2 teaspoons salt
- ½ tablespoon lemon juice
- ½ cup water
- 1 small head cauliflower, broken into flowerets
- 2 tablespoons olive oil
- 1 tablespoon vinegar
- 1 avocado, peeled, pitted and sliced
- 1 slice boiled or baked ham, diced
  Lettuce leaves
- 1½ cups mayonnaise

Place one teaspoon of the salt, the lemon juice and water in a medium-size saucepan. Add cauliflower, cover and bring to a boil. Boil until cauliflower is tender, eight to ten minutes. Drain and set aside to cool thoroughly. Combine remaining salt, olive oil, vinegar, avocado and ham in a large bowl. Add cauliflower and toss to coat cauliflower. Arrange lettuce leaves on individual salad plates. Place cauliflower on lettuce. Spoon on mayonnaise. Makes 6 to 8 servings.

Col con Trozos de Oro

Cabbage with Gold Nuggets

- 1 pound shredded red cabbage
- 1 small can chunk pineapple, drained
- 8 ounces shredded coconut, soaked for 15 minutes in cold water and drained
- ½ cup heavy cream
- 1 cup mayonnaise

Place cabbage, pineapple and coconut in a medium-size bowl. Toss lightly. Refrigerate for one hour. Prior to serving, whip cream until stiff in a chilled bowl. Fold in mayonnaise. Fold mixture into salad. Serve immediately. Makes 5 to 6 servings.

Vinegar and Oil Dressing

- 1 cup vegetable oil
- ⅓ cup wine or cider vinegar
- ½ teaspoon dry mustard
- ⅛ teaspoon cayenne
- ½ teaspoon salt
- ¼ teaspoon ground pepper

Combine all ingredients and mix well. Place in a covered container and chill at least one hour before using. Makes 1⅓ cups.

Rum Salad Dressing

- 9 tablespoons vegetable oil
- 3 tablespoons lime juice
- 3 tablespoons light rum
- 2 tablespoons brown sugar
- ½ teaspoon salt
- ¼ teaspoon freshly ground pepper

Combine all ingredients in a shaker. Shake until thoroughly mixed. Refrigerate until ready to use. Stir before using. Makes 1 cup.

Chili Mayonnaise

- 1 cup mayonnaise
- 1 teaspoon chili powder or hot chili powder
- ¼ teaspoon salt
- ¼ teaspoon white pepper
- 2 teaspoons lemon juice
- 1 green onion, chopped

Combine all ingredients in a medium-size mixing bowl. Place in a covered container and refrigerate until ready to use. Makes 1 cup.

Avocado Salad Dressing

- 1 large, ripe avocado, peeled, reserve seed
  Juice of 1 large lemon or 2 tablespoons lemon juice
- 1 small green pepper, seeded and chopped
- 1 small onion, chopped
- 1 cup mayonnaise
- ¼ teaspoon salt
- ¼ teaspoon Tabasco sauce
- ⅛ teaspoon white pepper

Cut avocado into chunks; sprinkle with lemon juice. Place avocado, pepper, onion, mayonnaise, salt, Tabasco and pepper into a blender or food processor. Blend until smooth; pour into a covered container. Place avocado seed in center of dressing. (Seed helps to retard color change.) Chill one hour before serving. Makes 2 cups.

Nopales with Tomatoes

2 tablespoons vegetable oil
2 tablespoons olive oil
1 large onion, chopped
1 16-ounce can tomatoes, drained and chopped
1 19-ounce can nopales, drained
½ teaspoon salt
¼ teaspoon pepper

Heat oils in a ten-inch skillet. Add onion and sauté for two minutes, stirring occasionally. Add remaining ingredients; mix well. Simmer, uncovered, for five minutes, or until vegetables are heated through. Makes 6 servings.

Corn Pudding

6 extra large eggs
½ cup milk
1 teaspoon granulated sugar
½ teaspoon salt
3 12-ounce cans whole kernel corn, drained
2 tablespoons all-purpose flour
2 tablespoons butter, melted

Preheat oven to 325°. Beat eggs until lemon-colored. Add milk, sugar and salt. Combine corn, flour and butter. Stir corn mixture into egg mixture. Pour into a buttered two-quart casserole. Bake fifty minutes. Makes 8 servings.

Colache *Mixed Vegetable Dish*

2 tablespoons butter
2 tablespoons vegetable oil
1 clove garlic, chopped
1 large onion, chopped
1½ cups cut green beans
¾ cup water
5 zucchini, cut into 1-inch pieces
3 large tomatoes, peeled, seeded and chopped
4 ears corn, peeled and cut into 1½-inch pieces
½ teaspoon salt
¼ teaspoon pepper

Heat butter and oil in a twelve-inch skillet. Add garlic and onion and sauté until onion is soft, about two minutes, stirring occasionally. Add remaining ingredients, except salt and pepper. Simmer, covered, fifteen minutes, or until beans are tender. Add salt and pepper; mix lightly. Makes 6 servings.

After handling strong-smelling foods, such as onion or garlic, sprinkle celery salt or celery seed on hands; rub and rinse. Odor will disappear.

Sweet Potatoes and Pineapple

Good as a vegetable or a dessert.

1 16-ounce can sweet potatoes, drained and mashed
1½ cups crushed pineapple, drained, reserve juice
½ cup packed dark brown sugar
½ cup granulated sugar
2 teaspoons grated orange rind
¼ cup chopped walnuts

In a heavy two-quart saucepan, combine all ingredients. Simmer for thirty minutes. Pour into an oiled loaf pan or individual dishes; chill for at least one hour. Unmold from loaf pan. Makes 6 servings.

Potatoes and Eggs

4 tablespoons vegetable oil
4 tablespoons olive oil
2 cloves garlic, minced
1 large onion, chopped
3 medium potatoes, peeled and cut into ½-inch cubes
6 extra large eggs, lightly beaten
3 tablespoons water
½ teaspoon salt
¼ teaspoon white pepper

Heat both oils in a ten-inch skillet. Add garlic and onion; sauté for one minute, stirring occasionally. Add potatoes and sauté until the potatoes are tender. Pour off excess oil. In a mixing bowl, combine eggs, water, salt and pepper; beat lightly. Pour egg mixture into skillet. Scramble lightly until the eggs have set. Eggs should have a custard-like quality. Serve hot with a prepared chili sauce. Makes 3 to 4 servings.

Corn Fritters

1 12-ounce can whole kernel corn
¼ cup milk
1 cup all-purpose flour
2 teaspoons baking powder
1 extra large egg, lightly beaten
2 cups vegetable oil

In a large mixing bowl, combine all ingredients, except oil. Set aside for twenty minutes. Heat the oil in an eight-inch skillet. For each fritter, carefully drop one tablespoonful of batter into the oil. Cook until golden brown, about one minute. Remove fritters with a slotted spoon; drain on paper toweling. Makes about 20 fritters.

Chayotes with Cream Sauce

    6 large chayotes
    6 tablespoons butter
    4 tablespoons all-purpose flour
    1 pint half and half
    ½ teaspoon salt
    ½ teaspoon pepper
    4 ounces Monterey Jack cheese, shredded
    1 2-ounce jar pimiento

Place chayotes in a three-quart saucepan; cover with water. Cook over medium heat, uncovered, until chayotes are tender. Drain, peel and cut into one-half-inch cubes; set aside. Melt butter in the same saucepan. Add flour and mix well. Slowly stir in cream, stirring constantly. Simmer until sauce begins to thicken, stirring constantly. Add salt, pepper, cheese, pimiento and chayote; mix well. Heat until the cheese melts, stirring frequently. Makes 12 servings.

Zucchini Patties

    3 cups grated zucchini
    1 small onion, minced
    1 small carrot, grated
    ¾ cup all-purpose flour
    ¾ teaspoon baking powder
    1 extra large egg, lightly beaten
    ½ teaspoon salt
    ¼ teaspoon white pepper
    3 tablespoons butter
    3 tablespoons vegetable oil

Combine all ingredients, except butter and oil, in a large mixing bowl; mix well. Heat butter and oil in a large skillet. Shape zucchini mixture into patties. Fry until golden brown on each side. Makes 8 to 10 servings.

Lima Beans with Onions

    4 tablespoons vegetable oil
    2 cloves garlic, minced
    2 large onions, sliced
    1 pound dried lima beans, soaked overnight and
        drained or 2 10-ounce packages frozen beans,
        cooked and drained
    ½ teaspoon salt
    ¼ teaspoon pepper
    ½ cup beef bouillon

Heat oil in a Dutch oven. Add garlic and onion, and sauté for two minutes, stirring occasionally. Add remaining ingredients. Simmer, uncovered, for fifty minutes. Gently stir three times. Serve hot. Makes 8 servings.

Stewed Corn

    ¼ cup butter
    8 ears corn or 3 12-ounce cans whole kernel corn,
        drained
    2 tablespoons bacon drippings
    ½ teaspoon salt
    ¼ teaspoon white pepper
    1 teaspoon granulated sugar

Melt butter in a small saucepan. Scrape corn off cobs. Place corn in skillet. Simmer for twenty minutes, stirring occasionally. Add remaining ingredients and simmer for five minutes. If the corn mixture becomes too thick, add a small amount of water. Makes 6 servings.

Tangy Green Beans with Pimientos

    3 slices bacon, fried, drained and crumbled,
        reserve drippings
    3 cloves garlic, minced
    1 large onion, chopped
    ¼ cup red wine vinegar
    1 teaspoon sugar
    ½ teaspoon salt
    ½ teaspoon pepper
    1 2-ounce jar pimiento, chopped
    ½ teaspoon cumin seed
    1½ pounds cooked green beans

Heat bacon drippings in a large skillet. Add garlic and onion and sauté for two minutes, stirring occasionally. Add bacon. Stir in wine vinegar, sugar, salt, pepper, pimiento and cumin seed. Add beans; mix gently. Cover and simmer for five minutes. Makes 6 servings.

Stuffed Zucchini

    12 small to medium zucchini
    3 tablespoons vegetable oil
    2 cloves garlic, minced
    1 medium onion, chopped
    ½ cup dry bread crumbs
    1 medium tomato, peeled, seeded and chopped
    ½ teaspoon oregano
    ¼ teaspoon ground cumin
    ½ teaspoon salt

Cut zucchini in half lengthwise. Scoop out pulp; set aside. Heat oil in a skillet. Add garlic and onion; sauté for two minutes, stirring occasionally. Add zucchini pulp, bread crumbs, tomato, oregano, cumin and salt; mix well. Simmer for one minute. Spoon mixture into shells. Place on a lightly oiled baking sheet. Bake at 350° for ten minutes, or until zucchini are thoroughly heated. Makes 12 servings.

Marinated Garbanzo Beans

4 15-ounce cans garbanzo beans, drained
¼ cup lemon juice
¼ cup red wine vinegar
¾ cup vegetable oil
2 cloves garlic, minced
1 large onion, chopped
5 ribs celery, chopped
1 large red pepper, seeded and chopped
¼ teaspoon salt
¼ teaspoon pepper
½ teaspoon basil

Place beans in a large salad bowl. Combine lemon juice, vinegar, oil and garlic in a small bowl. Toss dressing with beans. Add onion, celery and pepper. Sprinkle salt, pepper and basil over salad. Chill for one hour before serving. Toss before serving. Makes 12 servings.

Plantains in Mole Sauce

2 ripe plantains, peeled
3 tablespoons vegetable oil
1 cup Mole Sauce (Recipe on page 52)

Slice plantains diagonally in two-inch pieces. Heat oil in a medium-size skillet. Fry plantains about three minutes on each side, or until golden brown. Remove to a serving platter. Heat Mole Sauce in small saucepan for one minute, stirring constantly. Pour sauce over plantains. Serve hot. Makes 6 servings.

Marinated String Beans

2 pounds string beans, trimmed
2 teaspoons salt
1 large onion, thinly sliced
1 15-ounce can garbanzo beans, drained
⅓ cup olive oil
5 tablespoons red wine vinegar
½ teaspoon salt
¼ teaspoon pepper

Place beans in a large saucepan; cover with water and add salt. Bring to a boil; reduce to moderate heat and cook for four minutes, until beans are cooked, but still crisp. Drain and place beans in a salad bowl. Add remaining ingredients; toss to coat evenly. Chill for one hour before serving. Makes 10 to 12 servings.

Squash with Brown Sugar

3½ pounds banana squash
1¼ cups firmly packed brown sugar
1 cup water

Wash squash, remove seeds and cut into 1½-inch pieces. Place squash in a two-quart saucepan. Add sugar and water. Cover and simmer for fifty minutes, or until tender. Uncover and cook for ten minutes until the syrup begins to thicken. Serve with cream. Serve at breakfast or as a vegetable. Makes 6 servings.

Stuffed Peppers

16 sweet finger peppers, slit and seeded
½ pound Monterey Jack cheese, cut into ½-inch strips
3 jumbo eggs, separated
4 tablespoons all-purpose flour
2 cups vegetable oil
Flour
4 large tomatoes, peeled and chopped
1 small onion, chopped
1 chicken bouillon cube
½ teaspoon crushed oregano leaves
½ teaspoon salt
¼ teaspoon pepper
4 ounces Cheddar cheese, shredded

Stuff each pepper with Monterey Jack cheese, dividing cheese evenly among peppers. Beat egg whites until soft peaks form. Beat egg yolks until lemony yellow; add to egg whites. Sprinkle flour over egg mixture; fold together. Heat oil in a heavy, medium-size skillet. Coat peppers with flour. Dip peppers into egg batter. Fry in oil until golden on all sides. Drain on paper toweling. Heat oven to 350°. In medium-size saucepan, combine tomatoes, onion, bouillon, oregano, salt and pepper. Simmer, covered, for three minutes, stirring occasionally. Place peppers in a shallow baking dish. Spoon sauce over tops of peppers. Sprinkle cheese over sauce. Bake, uncovered, for fifteen minutes. Serve hot. Makes 8 servings.

Zucchini with Corn

4 tablespoons vegetable oil
1½ pounds zucchini, thinly sliced
1 large tomato, peeled and chopped
1 large onion, chopped
½ teaspoon salt
⅛ teaspoon pepper
1 16-ounce can white corn, drained, reserving half the liquid
½ pound Monterey Jack cheese, shredded

Heat oil in a two-quart saucepan. Add remaining ingredients. Bring to a boil; reduce heat and simmer until cheese melts, stirring frequently. Serve hot. Makes 6 to 8 servings.

Carne (Meat)

Albondigas *Meatballs with Tomato Sauce*

- ¼ pound bacon
- 1 pound ground beef
- ½ teaspoon salt
- ¼ teaspoon ground cumin
- ½ teaspoon garlic powder
- 2 extra large eggs, lightly beaten
- ½ cup all-purpose flour
- 6 tablespoons vegetable oil
- 2 cups Tomato Sauce (Recipe on page 52)

Fry bacon in a heavy skillet until crisp; drain and crumble. Place bacon in a large mixing bowl. Add ground beef, salt, cumin, garlic powder and eggs; mix well. Shape into walnut-size balls. Place on an oiled plate. Refrigerate for one hour. Roll each meatball in flour. Heat oil in a twelve-inch skillet. Fry meatballs until done, turning to brown all sides. Arrange in a shallow serving dish and cover with heated Tomato Sauce. Makes 4 to 5 servings.

Beef and Cheese Enchiladas

Filling

- 3 tablespoons vegetable oil
- 1 large onion, chopped
- 1 pound ground beef, browned
- ½ teaspoon salt
- ½ pound Cheddar cheese, grated
- 1 10-ounce can enchilada sauce

Heat oil in a medium-size skillet. Add onion and sauté for two minutes or until soft, stirring occasionally. Place onion in a large mixing bowl. Add remaining ingredients and mix well. Set mixture aside.

Tortillas

- ½ cup vegetable oil or lard
- 12 corn tortillas

Heat oil in a medium-size skillet. Using tongs to hold tortillas, fry for five seconds on each side. Drain on paper toweling.

Sauce

- 1 10-ounce can enchilada sauce
- 2 15-ounce cans tomato sauce

Combine both sauces in a mixing bowl; mix well.

Assemble

- ½ pound grated Monterey Jack cheese

Preheat oven to 350°. Spoon two tablespoons Filling on each tortilla. Roll up each tortilla. If there is any remaining Filling, add to the Sauce. Place tortillas, seam side down, in a greased 9 x 13-inch casserole. Pour Sauce over enchiladas. Sprinkle cheese over Sauce. Bake, uncovered, for twenty minutes, or until thoroughly heated. Makes 6 servings.

Carne Asada *Pot Roast*

- 1 5-pound chuck roast or eye of round
- ½ teaspoon salt
- ¼ teaspoon pepper
- 5 tablespoons vegetable oil
- 2 medium onions, chopped
- 2 cloves garlic, minced
- 2 green peppers, seeded and cut into ½-inch strips
- 4 large carrots, peeled and sliced
- 5 potatoes, peeled and cut into quarters
- ¾ cup dry red wine

Season roast with salt and pepper. Heat oil in a Dutch oven. Brown meat lightly on both sides. Add remaining ingredients. Add water to cover meat. Cover and simmer for ninety minutes, or until meat is tender. Serve with tortillas, Red Chili Sauce and Green Chili Sauce (Recipes on pages 52 and 53). Makes 4 to 5 servings.

Red Chili

- 3 tablespoons bacon drippings
- 1 clove garlic, minced
- 1 medium onion, chopped
- 2½ pounds chuck steak, shredded
- 3 tablespoons chili powder
- 1 teaspoon ground red chili peppers
- 1 teaspoon salt
- 1 teaspoon paprika
- ½ teaspoon oregano
- 1 cup sour cream

Heat bacon drippings in a twelve-inch skillet. Add garlic and onion and sauté until onion is soft, about two minutes, stirring occasionally. Add remaining ingredients; stir. Simmer uncovered, one hour, until beef is tender, stirring occasionally. Taste for seasoning. Serve with a dollop of sour cream. Makes 8 servings.

Easy Beef Enchiladas
Filling

- 3 tablespoons vegetable oil
- 1 large onion, chopped
- 1½ pounds ground beef
- ½ teaspoon salt
- ½ teaspoon ground cumin

Heat oil in a ten-inch skillet. Add onion and sauté for two minutes, stirring occasionally. Add beef, salt and cumin; brown beef, stirring occasionally. Cool.

Tortillas

- 16 5½-inch corn tortillas
- 1 cup vegetable oil

Heat oil in an eight-inch skillet. Using tongs to hold tortillas, fry for five seconds on each side; drain on paper toweling.

Sauce

- 2 10-ounce cans enchilada sauce
- 1 4-ounce can mild green peppers, rinsed, drained, seeded and chopped

Combine enchilada sauce and green peppers in a large mixing bowl.

Assemble

- ½ pound Monterey Jack cheese, grated

Preheat oven to 350°. Place two tablespoons Filling on each tortilla. Sprinkle cheese on top. Roll up. Place enchiladas, seam side down, in an oiled 9 x 13-inch casserole. Pour sauce over enchiladas. Bake, uncovered, for twenty minutes. Makes 8 servings.

Enchiladas with Green Sauce
Filling

- 3 tablespoons vegetable oil
- 1 clove garlic, minced
- 2 medium onions, minced
- 1¾ pounds ground beef
- 1 large green pepper, seeded and chopped
- 1 tablespoon chili powder
- ½ teaspoon ground cumin
- ½ teaspoon crushed red pepper flakes
- ½ cup red wine

Heat oil in a ten-inch skillet. Add garlic and onion. Sauté until onion is soft, about two minutes, stirring occasionally. Add ground beef, green pepper, chili powder, cumin and red pepper flakes. Brown meat over moderate heat, stirring often. Stir in wine. Cool Filling. Set aside.

Tortillas

- 16 tortillas
- 1 cup vegetable oil

Heat oil in an eight-inch skillet. Using tongs to hold tortillas, fry for five seconds on each side. Drain on paper toweling.

Sauce

- 1 10-ounce can green tomatoes, drained and chopped
- 1 4-ounce can mild green peppers, rinsed, seeded, drained and chopped
- ½ cup chopped cilantro
- 2 cups chicken bouillon

Combine all ingredients in a large bowl. Refrigerate until ready to serve.

Assemble

- ½ pound Monterey Jack cheese, grated
- 2 cups sour cream

Preheat oven to 350°. Dip tortilla in sauce. Place two tablespoons Filling on each tortilla. Roll up. Place tortillas, seam side down, in an oiled 9 x 13-inch casserole. Pour remaining Sauce over enchiladas. Sprinkle cheese over top. Bake for twenty minutes, or until the cheese has melted. Spoon sour cream over top of enchiladas. Makes 8 servings.

Picadillo *Hash with Spices*

- 3 tablespoons vegetable oil
- 2 cloves garlic, minced
- 1 large onion, chopped
- 2 pounds ground beef
- 1 pound ground pork
- 2 large tomatoes, peeled, seeded and chopped
- 1 large apple, peeled and sliced
- ½ cup chopped almonds
- 1 teaspoon sugar
- ½ teaspoon salt
- ¼ teaspoon black pepper
- ½ cup raisins
- 2 teaspoons vinegar
- 1 tablespoon chili powder
- ½ teaspoon ground cumin
- ½ teaspoon cinnamon

Heat oil in a heavy twelve-inch skillet. Add garlic and onion. Sauté, stirring occasionally, until onion is soft, about two minutes. Add beef and pork and brown, stirring often. Drain excess fat. Add remaining ingredients; mix well. Simmer, uncovered, over low heat for twenty-five minutes, stirring occasionally. Serve with rice and refried beans. Makes 8 servings.

Green Chili con Carne

Meat with Green Chilies

- 3 tablespoons vegetable oil
- 2 medium onions, chopped
- 2½ pounds chuck steak or round steak, cut into ½-inch pieces
- ½ cup beef bouillon
- 1 canned jalapeno pepper, rinsed, seeded, chopped and drained
- 2 4-ounce cans mild green chilies, rinsed, seeded, chopped and drained
- ½ teaspoon salt
- ½ teaspoon ground cumin
- 2 tablespoons cornstarch
- 1 cup sour cream

Heat oil in a Dutch oven. Add onion and sauté for two minutes, or until onion is soft, stirring occasionally. Add meat; brown over moderate heat, stirring occasionally. Add remaining ingredients, except cornstarch and sour cream. Cover and simmer for fifty minutes, or until meat is tender, stirring occasionally. Remove four tablespoons gravy and place in a cup. Add the cornstarch; mix. Return to Dutch oven and mix well. Continue simmering until the gravy begins to thicken, stirring constantly. Serve in deep bowls garnished with a dollop of sour cream. Serve with beans and tortillas. Makes 6 servings.

Chopped Beef Tongue

- 2 tablespoons vegetable oil
- 1 large onion, chopped
- 2½ cups chopped, cooked beef tongue
- 1 4-ounce can mild chilies, drained and chopped
- 1 large tomato, peeled, seeded and chopped
- ½ teaspoon salt
- ¼ teaspoon black pepper

Heat oil in a twelve-inch skillet. Add onion and sauté until soft, about two minutes, stirring often. Combine chopped tongue with onion. Add remaining ingredients and mix thoroughly. Cover and simmer for ten minutes. Serve hot with a tossed salad, or with eggs for breakfast. Makes 4 servings.

Beef Tongue with Sauce

- 4 pounds beef tongue, washed
- 4 cloves garlic, crushed
- 4 bay leaves
- 2 tablespoons salt
  Water

Place tongue in a five-quart stockpot. Add garlic, bay leaves, and salt. Add enough water to cover. Bring to a boil. Cover and simmer for four hours, or until tongue is soft. Remove tongue from pot, rinse with cold water and remove the skin. Cool tongue and cut into thin slices. Cover with Sauce. Serve hot with rice. Makes 5 to 6 servings.

Sauce

- 3 tablespoons vegetable oil
- 1 medium onion, chopped
- 3 ribs celery, chopped
- 1 35-ounce can tomatoes, drained and chopped
- ½ teaspoon salt
- ¼ teaspoon pepper
- 2 tablespoons red wine vinegar
- 2 tablespoons granulated sugar

Heat oil in a medium-size saucepan. Add onion and celery; sauté for two minutes or until soft, stirring occasionally. Add tomatoes, salt, pepper, vinegar and sugar to onion; mix well. Simmer for one minute; cool. Place in a covered container and refrigerate until ready to serve. Heat before serving.

Tamale Pie

- 2 tablespoons vegetable oil
- 1 large onion, chopped
- ½ teaspoon garlic powder
- 1 pound ground beef
- 1 15-ounce can tomato sauce
- 1 12-ounce can whole kernel corn, drained
- 1 cup chopped black olives
- ½ teaspoon salt
- 2 teaspoons chili powder
- 2 cups grated Monterey Jack cheese
- ¾ cup yellow cornmeal
- ¼ teaspoon salt
- 2 cups water
- 2 tablespoons bacon drippings

Heat oil in a twelve-inch skillet. Add onion and garlic powder; sauté for two minutes, stirring occasionally. Add ground beef and brown, stirring often; drain excess fat. Add tomato sauce, corn, black olives, salt and chili powder. Simmer uncovered, for fifteen minutes. Add cheese and stir until cheese is melted. Pour into an eleven-inch pie plate. Heat oven to 375°. Combine cornmeal, salt and water in a medium-size saucepan. Cook over moderate heat, stirring constantly until cornmeal mixture begins to thicken. Stir in bacon drippings. Arrange cornmeal mixture over meat. Bake for thirty-five minutes. Serve hot. Makes 6 servings.

Company Chili

- 3 tablespoons vegetable oil
- 2 cloves garlic, minced
- 2 large onions, chopped
- 2 pounds ground chuck
- ½ teaspoon salt
- ¼ teaspoon Tabasco sauce
- ⅛ teaspoon black pepper
- ¼ teaspoon chili powder
- ½ teaspoon ground cumin
- 2 6-ounce cans tomato paste
- 2 16-ounce cans tomatoes, drained
- 2 15-ounce cans red kidney beans, drained

Heat oil in a four-quart saucepan. Add garlic and onion. Sauté until onion is soft, stirring occasionally. Add ground meat and salt; brown meat. Add Tabasco, pepper, chili powder, cumin, tomato paste and tomatoes. Simmer, covered, one hour, stirring occasionally. Add kidney beans. Simmer covered, fifteen minutes. Makes 8 servings.

Chili-Pork Enchiladas

Filling

- 3 tablespoons vegetable oil
- 1 clove garlic, minced
- 1 large onion, chopped
- 1½ pounds ground pork
- ½ teaspoon salt
- 2 dried cascabel chilies
- 1 4-ounce can mild peppers, rinsed, seeded, chopped and drained

Heat oil in a ten-inch skillet. Add garlic and onion and sauté for two minutes, or until onion is soft, stirring occasionally. Add pork and salt; brown pork, stirring occasionally. Place cascabel chilies in a one-quart saucepan, cover with water and simmer for four minutes. Drain; remove skin, seeds and stem. Add cascabel chilies and mild peppers to pork; stir to combine. Cook for two minutes. Remove from heat and set aside.

Tortillas

- 16 7-inch corn tortillas
- 1 cup vegetable oil

Heat oil in an eight-inch skillet. Using tongs to hold tortillas, fry for five seconds on each side. Drain on paper toweling.

Sauce

- 3 cups tomato sauce
- 1 clove garlic, minced
- 1 medium onion, chopped
- ½ teaspoon granulated sugar

Combine all ingredients in a large mixing bowl and mix well.

Assemble

- 1 cup grated Longhorn cheese

Preheat oven to 350°. Place two tablespoons Filling on each tortilla. Roll up. Place tortillas, seam side down, in an oiled 9 x 13-inch casserole. Pour Sauce over enchiladas. Sprinkle cheese over top. Bake, uncovered, for twenty minutes, or until the enchiladas are heated and the cheese has melted. Makes 8 servings.

Pork Spareribs

- 3½ pounds pork spareribs
- 2 tablespoons vegetable oil
- 1 tablespoon olive oil
- 3 cloves garlic, minced
- 1 teaspoon salt
- ½ teaspoon pepper
- 1 teaspoon oregano
- 1 teaspoon chopped cilantro
- 1 large onion, chopped
- 3 tablespoons orange juice
- 2½ cups Veracruz Sauce (Recipe on page 52)

Trim fat from spareribs; slice into individual ribs. Place in a shallow baking pan. Combine oils, garlic, salt, pepper, oregano, cilantro, onion and orange juice. Spread marinade over ribs. Let stand at room temperature for three hours. Preheat oven to 350°. Cover ribs with Veracruz Sauce. Bake for two hours or until tender, turning ribs occasionally. Serve with additional sauce. Makes 4 to 5 servings.

Leg of Lamb

- 2 cloves garlic, minced
- 1 small onion, minced
- 1 teaspoon oregano
- 1 tablespoon chili powder
- ½ teaspoon ground cumin
- ½ teaspoon salt
- ¼ teaspoon pepper
- 1 6-pound leg of lamb
- 3 tablespoons wine vinegar
- 3 tablespoons vegetable oil

Combine garlic, onion, oregano, chili powder, cumin, salt and pepper in a small mixing bowl; mix lightly. Rub over lamb. Combine vinegar and oil; sprinkle over lamb. Refrigerate lamb for one day. Preheat oven to 350°. Place lamb in a roasting pan. Bake, uncovered, for two hours or fifteen minutes per pound. Makes 8 servings.

Chorizo

1 pound ground pork
¾ teaspoon oregano
3 tablespoons red wine vinegar
2 cloves garlic, minced
2 tablespoons chili powder
½ teaspoon black pepper
¾ teaspoon salt
¼ teaspoon ground cumin

Combine pork, oregano, vinegar, garlic and chili powder in a large mixing bowl. Add pepper, salt and cumin. Mix well. Shape into patties, fill casings or place in a covered container and refrigerate. Sausage will keep for one week. Makes 1 pound chorizo.

Barbara's Chorizo

1 pound ground pork
1 medium onion, minced
1 clove garlic, minced
¾ teaspoon oregano
¾ teaspoon ground coriander
2 tablespoons white vinegar
1 teaspoon salt
½ teaspoon black pepper
½ teaspoon cinnamon
½ teaspoon ground cumin

Combine all ingredients in a large mixing bowl; mix well. Shape into patties, fill casings or place in a covered container and refrigerate. Sausage will keep for one week. Makes 1 pound chorizo.

Beef Tacos

3 tablespoons vegetable oil
1 medium onion, chopped
1 pound ground beef
1 teaspoon chili powder
½ teaspoon oregano
½ teaspoon ground cumin
¼ teaspoon pepper
12 corn tortillas or taco shells
1 cup chopped onion

Heat oil in a skillet. Add onion and sauté for two minutes, stirring occasionally. Add beef, chili powder, oregano, cumin and pepper. Sauté over medium heat until beef is browned. Place two tablespoons filling in each taco. Serve with chopped onion, and Thick Red Chili Sauce (Recipe on page 52) or taco sauce. Makes 12 tacos.

Country Pork Ribs

2 dried ancho chilies
2 tablespoons vegetable oil
2 cloves garlic, minced
1 large onion, chopped
3½ pounds country-style ribs,
    cut into individual ribs
2 cups water
2 cups beef bouillon
1 4-ounce can mild green chilies, rinsed, drained,
    seeded and chopped
2 whole tomatoes, peeled and chopped
1 teaspoon salt
½ cup red wine vinegar
½ teaspoon ground cumin
1 teaspoon chopped parsley

Place ancho chilies in a one-quart sauce pan and cover with water. Bring to a boil; reduce heat. Cover and simmer for four minutes or until the chilies are soft. Drain, seed and remove stems from chilies. Set aside. Heat oil in a four-quart stockpot. Add garlic and onion and sauté until onion is soft, about two minutes, stirring occasionally. Add ribs, water and bouillon. Add more water or bouillon, if necessary, to cover ribs. Bring to a boil; reduce heat. Cover and simmer for fifty minutes, stirring occasionally, until ribs are tender. Place chilies and remaining ingredients in a blender or food processor and puree. Drain ribs and place in a broiler pan. Cover with the puree. Broil for six minutes on each side. Serve with rice and beans. Makes 4 to 5 servings.

How to Make Taco Shells

To make taco shells from tortillas, heat one cup vegetable oil or lard to 375° in a skillet. Place tortilla in hot oil and fry for ten seconds. Using tongs, fold tortilla in half and fry, holding edges apart to form a shell. Fry until crisp, turning once. Drain on paper toweling.

To make soft taco shells, heat tortillas in an ungreased skillet; fill and roll up. To warm tacos, heat in a 350° oven for fifteen minutes.

Lamb Stew

    4 tablespoons lard or vegetable oil
    2 pounds lamb, cut into 1-inch pieces
    ½ teaspoon garlic powder
    2 large onions, sliced
    2 green peppers, seeded and cut into ½-inch strips
    6 ribs celery, chopped
    1 teaspoon salt
    ½ teaspoon Tabasco sauce
    ½ teaspoon cumin seed
    ½ cup catsup
    5 large tomatoes, peeled, seeded and chopped

Heat lard or oil in a Dutch oven. Brown meat over moderate heat, stirring occasionally. Add remaining ingredients, except tomatoes. Reduce heat and simmer, uncovered, forty-five minutes, or until lamb is tender. Add tomatoes; cover and simmer fifteen minutes. Serve with rice. Makes 4 servings.

Pork Tablecloth Stainer

    2½ to 3 pounds boneless pork loin,
        cut into 1-inch cubes
    ½ teaspoon oregano
    2 cloves garlic, crushed
    2 tablespoons vegetable oil
    1 large onion, chopped
    1 green pepper, cut into ½-inch strips
    ¾ cup almonds
    3 cups beef bouillon
    ¼ teaspoon salt
    ¼ teaspoon cinnamon
    ¼ teaspoon allspice
    1 large ripe plantain, sliced
    2 medium bananas, sliced
    2 tart apples, cored, peeled and cubed
    1 8-ounce can pineapple chunks, drained

Place pork in a Dutch oven and cover with water. Add oregano and garlic; cover and simmer for one hour. Drain; reserve stock. Return pork to Dutch oven. Heat oil in a ten-inch skillet. Add onion, pepper and almonds; heat for one minute, stirring occasionally. Remove onion, pepper and almonds to a blender or a food processor. Place one cup of the bouillon, salt, cinnamon, and allspice in the blender; puree. Stir in remaining bouillon. Arrange plantain, bananas, apples and pineapple over pork. Spoon on sauce; cover and simmer for twenty-five to thirty minutes. Serve hot with fruit salad. Makes 5 to 6 servings.

Spicy Pork Enchiladas
Filling

    3 tablespoons vegetable oil
    2 cloves garlic, minced
    1 medium onion, chopped
    1 pound ground pork
    2 teaspoons all-purpose flour
    ¼ cup beef bouillon
    2 teaspoons chili powder
    ½ teaspoon red pepper flakes
    ½ teaspoon salt

Heat oil in twelve-inch skillet. Add garlic and onion and sauté until soft, about two minutes, stirring occasionally. Add pork, sprinkle with flour and brown, stirring occasionally. Add bouillon, chili powder, red pepper flakes and salt; stir to combine. Remove from heat. Set aside.

Tortillas

    16 flour tortillas
    ½ cup vegetable oil

Heat oil in medium-size skillet. Using tongs to hold tortillas, fry for five seconds on each side to soften. Drain on paper toweling.

Sauce

    2 tablespoons vegetable oil
    2 cloves garlic, minced
    8 green onions, chopped
    1 35-ounce can tomatoes, drained, seeded
        and chopped
    2 tablespoons wine vinegar
    1 teaspoon granulated sugar
    1 4-ounce can hot green chili peppers, rinsed,
        drained, seeded and chopped
    ½ teaspoon salt

Heat oil in a two-quart saucepan. Add garlic and onion and sauté for two minutes, or until onion is soft, stirring occasionally. Stir in remaining ingredients and simmer for three minutes, stirring occasionally. Place in a covered container. Refrigerate until ready to use.

Assemble

    2 cups grated Longhorn cheese
    2 cups sliced red radishes

Preheat oven to 350°. Place two tablespoons Filling on each tortilla and sprinkle with grated cheese. Roll up tortilla. Place tortillas, seam-side down, in a buttered shallow 9 x 13-inch casserole. Pour Sauce over enchiladas. Sprinkle on remaining cheese. Garnish with sliced radishes. Makes 16 enchiladas.

Enchiladas Suizas
Enchiladas with Sour Cream

Filling
- 4 cups chopped, cooked chicken
- 1 large onion, chopped
- 1 cup heavy cream

Combine all ingredients in a large mixing bowl; set aside.

Tortillas
- ½ cup vegetable oil
- 16 corn tortillas

Heat oil in a medium-size skillet. Using tongs to hold tortillas, fry for five seconds on each side. Drain on paper toweling.

Sauce
- 1 clove garlic, minced
- 6 large tomatoes, peeled, seeded and chopped
- ½ teaspoon crushed oregano
- ¼ teaspoon salt
- ¼ teaspoon black pepper
- 1 cup sour cream

Combine garlic, tomatoes, oregano, salt and pepper in blender or food processor; mix well. Blend in sour cream. Place in covered container and refrigerate until ready to use.

Assemble
- 1 cup sour cream

Preheat oven to 350°. Dip tortillas in sauce. Place three tablespoons Filling on each tortilla. Roll up each tortilla. Place, seam side down, in a shallow 9 x 13-inch casserole. Pour remaining Sauce over enchiladas. Bake, uncovered, for twenty minutes. Garnish each with two tablespoons sour cream. Makes 8 servings.

Chicken Enchiladas
Filling
- 3 tablespoons vegetable oil
- 1 large onion, chopped
- 2 cups cooked, diced chicken
- ¼ teaspoon salt
- ⅛ teaspoon white pepper
- 1½ cups cottage cheese

Heat oil in a medium-size skillet. Add onion and sauté until soft, stirring occasionally. Add chicken, salt and pepper. Heat chicken thoroughly, stirring frequently. Remove from heat, stir in cottage cheese.

Tortillas
- 12 corn tortillas
- ½ cup vegetable oil

Heat oil in medium-size skillet. Using tongs to hold tortillas, fry for five seconds on each side. Drain on paper toweling.

Sauce
- 2 cups canned tomato sauce
- ½ cup sliced green olives

In a medium-size mixing bowl, combine tomato sauce and olives.

Assemble
Preheat oven to 350°. Dip tortilla in sauce. Place 1½ teaspoons Filling on each tortilla; roll up. Place tortillas, seam side down, in a greased 9 x 13-inch casserole. Top with Sauce. Bake, uncovered, for twenty minutes. Makes 12 enchiladas.

Chicken with Spicy Walnut Sauce
- 3 tablespoons olive oil
- 2 cloves garlic, minced
- 1 large onion, chopped
- 1 5½-pound chicken, cooked, boned and skinned
- ½ cup chicken broth
- ½ teaspoon salt
- ¼ teaspoon white pepper
- ½ cup bread crumbs
- 2 cups heavy cream
- 1 4-ounce can hot or mild peppers, rinsed, drained seeded and chopped
- 1 cup chopped walnuts
- ¼ teaspoon cinnamon
- 6 medium potatoes, peeled, boiled and sliced

Heat oil in a ten- or twelve-inch skillet. Add garlic and onion and sauté for two minutes, stirring occasionally, until onion is soft. Add chicken, broth, salt and pepper. Cook for three minutes, stirring frequently. Combine bread crumbs, cream and peppers in a large mixing bowl. Stir in walnuts and cinnamon. Line a serving casserole with sliced potatoes. Arrange chicken over potatoes. Pour sauce over chicken. Bake, uncovered, at 350° for fifteen minutes. Makes 4 to 5 servings.

To increase refrigerator shelf life of pimientos and olives, pour a thin layer of salad oil on top.

Chicken Tamales

28 fresh corn husks, silk removed
⅓ cup lard or vegetable shortening
1½ cups masa harina
¼ teaspoon salt
¾ cup warm water
1 cup cooked chicken, minced
½ cup grated Monterey Jack cheese
½ teaspoon garlic powder

Trim edges of corn husks two inches from the top and two inches from the bottom. Wash. Place husks in a large mixing bowl and cover with hot water. Let stand for one-half hour before using. Beat lard until light and fluffy in a small mixing bowl. Combine masa harina, salt and warm water in a medium mixing bowl. Add lard; mix until light and smooth. Drain husks. Lay two corn husks side by side, one with the wide end up and the other with the wide end down. Overlap edges and seal with masa harina. In center of husks, spread three tablespoons of masa harina to form a 3 x 5-inch rectangle. Combine chicken, cheese and garlic powder in a medium-size mixing bowl. Top masa harina with two tablespoons of filling. Roll up, jelly-roll fashion; fold one end under and seal with masa harina or tie with string. Leave top side of tamale open. Arrange in a steamer with the open end facing up. Steam for fifty minutes.* Carefully uncover steamer. When dough comes away from the husks, the tamales should be done. Makes 14 tamales.

Tamales can be frozen, wrapped in aluminum foil. Thaw before reheating. Reheat in a preheated 350° oven.

*If you do not have a steamer, invert a heatproof soup bowl in a Dutch oven. Place a dinner plate over the soup bowl. Pour water under the plate.

Chicken with Raisins and Almonds

4 tablespoons vegetable oil
2 cloves garlic, minced
1 large onion, chopped
½ teaspoon salt
  Juice of 1 small lemon
1 3-pound roasting chicken, cut into 8 pieces
3 large tomatoes, peeled and chopped
½ cup raisins
½ cup almonds
½ cup sliced green olives
2 cups chicken bouillon

Heat oil in a Dutch oven. Add garlic and onion and sauté until soft, about two minutes, stirring occasionally. Sprinkle salt and lemon juice over chicken. Brown chicken on all sides. Add tomatoes, raisins, almonds, olives and bouillon; mix well. Simmer, uncovered, for thirty minutes over moderate heat or until chicken is tender. Serve in a deep bowl with white rice and tortillas. Makes 6 servings.

Chicken in Wine

1 3-pound chicken, cut into serving pieces
¼ cup vegetable oil
½ cup olive oil
½ cup red wine vinegar
1 clove garlic, minced
1 medium onion, thinly sliced
2 bay leaves
½ teaspoon oregano
½ teaspoon salt
¼ teaspoon pepper
3 tablespoons bacon drippings or vegetable oil
1 large onion, chopped
3 medium zucchini, cut into 1-inch pieces
3 cups dry red wine

Place chicken in a large mixing bowl. Combine oils, vinegar, garlic, onion, bay leaves, oregano, salt and pepper; sprinkle over the chicken. Marinate in refrigerator for six hours. Heat bacon drippings in a Dutch oven. Add onion and sauté for two minutes, stirring occasionally. Add zucchini, wine and chicken. Simmer, covered, for one hour or until the chicken is tender. Makes 4 to 5 servings.

Turkey with Sweet Bell Peppers

4 tablespoons vegetable oil or lard
2 cloves garlic, minced
3 medium onions, thinly sliced
3 large green and/or red bell peppers, seeded and sliced lengthwise
4 cups cubed, cooked turkey
¾ cup heavy cream
½ teaspoon oregano
½ teaspoon salt
¼ teaspoon white pepper
½ cup grated Monterey Jack cheese

Heat oil in a heavy twelve-inch skillet. Add garlic, onion and pepper slices. Sauté for two minutes, stirring occasionally. Add turkey and mix well. Stir in remaining ingredients. Simmer until the cheese begins to melt. Serve with fruit salad and tortillas. Makes 8 servings.

Chicken Tablecloth Stainers

    2 dried ancho chilies
    3 tablespoons vegetable oil
    1 2½-pound chicken, cut into serving pieces
    1 pound Chorizo or Italian sausage (Recipe
       on page 28)
    1 large onion, chopped
    4 tablespoons slivered almonds
    3 cups chicken bouillon
    ½ teaspoon cinnamon
    ¼ teaspoon salt
    2 large bananas, sliced
    1 8-ounce can pineapple chunks, drained

Place ancho chilies in a small saucepan; cover with water and boil for four minutes. Drain chilies; remove stems, seeds and skin. Set aside. Heat oil in a twelve-inch skillet. Brown chicken and chorizo; set aside. Drain four tablespoons of drippings from the skillet. Place drippings in a two-quart saucepan. Add onion and almonds and sauté for one minute, stirring occasionally. Add chilies, chicken bouillon, cinnamon and salt to onion mixture. Simmer for five minutes. Ladle sauce over chicken and chorizo. Simmer, uncovered, for thirty minutes. Add bananas and pineapple; stir and simmer fifteen minutes. Serve with fruit salad and rice. Makes 4 to 5 servings.

Sliced Chicken with Pumpkin Seed Mole

    4 dried ancho chilies
    ¾ cup pepitas
    1 10-ounce can green tomatoes, drained
       and chopped
    ½ cup loosely packed parsley
    ½ teaspoon salt
    3 tablespoons vegetable oil
    2 cloves garlic, minced
    1 cup chicken bouillon
    1 3-pound chicken, cooked and sliced

Lightly toast ancho chilies in an ungreased skillet. Place in a small saucepan, cover with water and cook for four minutes. Drain. Remove seeds and stem. Grind pepitas in a blender or food processor. Place ancho chilies, tomatoes, parsley and salt in the blender; puree. Heat oil in a small saucepan. Add garlic and sauté for thirty seconds. Stir in sauce and bouillon. Simmer for three minutes. Preheat oven to 375°. Arrange sliced chicken in a two-quart casserole. Ladle the sauce over chicken. Bake for fifteen minutes or until heated through. Serve with salad and warm tortillas. Makes 4 to 5 servings.

Duck with Almonds

    1 5-pound duck, roasted
    3 tablespoons vegetable oil
    2 tablespoons all-purpose flour
    2 cloves garlic, minced
    ¾ cup blanched, slivered almonds
    ½ cup raisins
    ½ teaspoon ground cumin
    ¼ teaspoon ground cloves
    1 extra large egg yolk
    2 cups chicken bouillon

In a one-quart saucepan, combine oil and flour; heat and stir until flour is absorbed. Add garlic, almonds, raisins, cumin, cloves and egg yolk; mix well. Slowly stir in chicken bouillon; simmer until sauce begins to thicken. Cut the duck into serving pieces and place in a baking pan. Preheat oven to 350°. Ladle sauce over duck. Bake for twenty minutes. Makes 4 servings.

Albondigas de Guajalote *Ground Turkey*

Serve as a main dish or make into small balls for appetizers.

    3   slices bread
    8¾ cups hot turkey or chicken broth
    3   cups chopped, cooked turkey or chicken
    3   eggs
    1½ teaspoons minced parsley
    1   teaspoon salt
    ¾   teaspoon ground coriander
    ¼   teaspoon ground cloves
        Pinch nutmeg
    ¼   cup dry sherry
    2   tablespoons butter
    ¾   cup ground almonds
    1   green pepper, seeded and chopped
    1   avocado, cut into cubes, optional

Soak bread in three-fourths cup of the hot broth; drain. Grind turkey and bread together. Add eggs and mix well. Add seasonings and mix well. Form into small balls. Bring remaining broth to a boil in a large saucepan. Stir in sherry. Add butter. Reduce heat to a simmer. Carefully drop turkey balls into simmering broth. Simmer for twenty minutes. Remove balls and set aside in a warm place. Bring broth to a boil. Continue boiling until broth is reduced to about half. Add almonds and continue boiling until mixture starts to thicken. Add green pepper. Return turkey to broth. Cook for seven to eight minutes, or until pepper is tender-crisp. Just prior to serving, add avocado. Makes 4 to 5 servings.

Chicken with Mole Sauce

    2 3½-pound chickens, cut into serving pieces
    1 large onion, sliced
    4 ground cloves
    3 bay leaves
       Water
    ¼ cup cooking oil

Place chicken parts in a stockpot. Add onion, cloves, bay leaves and water to cover. Bring to a boil; reduce heat and skim. Cook over moderate heat until chicken is almost cooked, about thirty minutes. Remove chicken, discard bay leaves, reserve stock. Preheat oven to 350°. Heat oil in a large skillet. Brown chicken on both sides. Remove chicken to one large or two medium casseroles; ladle Mole Sauce over chicken. Bake twenty minutes. Serve hot with white rice. Makes 8 to 10 servings.

Mole Sauce

    2 cloves garlic, minced
    1 medium onion, minced
    2 large tomatoes, peeled, seeded and chopped
    1 green pepper, seeded and chopped
    2 toasted tortillas, broken into crumbs
    ½ cup raisins
    ½ cup peanuts
    ¼ teaspoon ground allspice
    ¼ teaspoon cinnamon
    ¼ teaspoon ground cumin
    2 teaspoons chili powder
    1 teaspoon sesame seed
    1 tablespoon sugar
    3 tablespoons vegetable oil
    2 cups reserved chicken stock

Combine all ingredients, except vegetable oil and chicken stock, in large bowl; mix well. Heat oil in a medium-size saucepan. Add mixture and chicken stock. Cook over moderate heat for two minutes. Makes 4 cups.

Pollo en Cerveza *Chicken in Beer*

    6 tablespoons vegetable oil
    2 cloves garlic, minced
    2 large onions, chopped
    1 5-pound chicken, cut into 8 serving pieces
    ½ teaspoon salt
    ¼ teaspoon white pepper
    ½ cup whole green olives
    4 large tomatoes, peeled and quartered
    6 large potatoes, peeled and quartered
    3 sweet green peppers, seeded and sliced
    2 12-ounce cans Mexican or domestic beer

Heat oil in a Dutch oven. Add garlic and onion and sauté for two minutes, stirring occasionally, until onion is soft. Add chicken; sprinkle on salt and pepper. Add remaining ingredients. Simmer, uncovered, for one hour or until chicken is tender, stirring occasionally. Makes 4 to 5 servings.

Turkey-Almond Empanadas

This is a good recipe for leftover turkey.

Pastry

Use two packages ready-made empanada pastry circles, pie crust mix or the following recipe.

    1¾ cups all-purpose flour
    ¼   teaspoon salt
    4   tablespoons lard
    3   tablespoons butter
    5   to 7 tablespoons ice water
    1   extra large egg, lightly beaten
    1   tablespoon water

In a mixing bowl, combine flour, salt, lard and butter. Cut lard and butter into the flour using a pastry knife or a food processor. Add ice water, a teaspoon at a time, mixing until dough holds together. Cover with plastic wrap and refrigerate for thirty minutes before using. Roll out on a lightly floured board to one-eighth inch thickness. Cut into circles using a 3½- to 4-inch cookie cutter. Place a scant two teaspoonfuls of the filling in the center of each circle. Fold in half; crimp edges together. Preheat oven to 375°. Place empanadas on a baking sheet. Combine egg and water; brush over empanadas. Bake twenty-five minutes or until golden brown. Serve warm. Can be frozen and reheated to serve. Makes 23 to 24 empanadas.

Filling

    3   tablespoons vegetable oil
    1   clove garlic, minced
    1   small onion, minced
    1½ cups chopped, cooked turkey
    ⅓   cup blanched, slivered almonds
    ⅓   cup raisins
    ¼   teaspoon salt
    ⅛   teaspoon pepper

Heat oil in a ten-inch skillet. Add garlic and onion; sauté for two minutes. Add remaining ingredients, mixing well. Remove from heat and cool before filling the empanadas.

Spicy Chicken or Turkey Tacos

    3 tablespoons vegetable oil
    2 cloves garlic, minced
    1 medium onion, chopped
    1 sweet bell pepper, seeded and chopped
2½ cups chopped, cooked chicken or turkey
    ½ teaspoon salt
    ½ teaspoon red pepper flakes
   14 6-inch corn tortillas or taco shells (See page 28)
      Shredded lettuce
      Grated sharp Cheddar cheese

Heat oil in a skillet. Add garlic, onion and pepper and sauté for two minutes, stirring often. Add chicken, salt and red pepper flakes. Cook over medium heat until the chicken is warm, stirring occasionally. Fill each taco shell with two tablespoons filling. Serve garnished with lettuce and cheese. Makes 14 servings.

Chicken Tacos

    4 tablespoons vegetable oil
    4 green onions, chopped
    1 cup chopped celery
    2 cups chopped, cooked chicken
    1 4-ounce can mild green peppers, rinsed, drained, seeded, and chopped
   12 6-inch corn tortillas, or taco shells (See page 28)
      Shredded lettuce
      Guacamole Sauce, (Recipe on page 52)

Heat oil in a skillet. Add onion and celery and sauté for two minutes, stirring occasionally. Add chicken and cook over medium heat two minutes, until chicken is heated through, stirring occasionally. Fill each taco shell with two tablespoons filling. Serve garnished with shredded lettuce and Guacamole Sauce. Makes 12 servings.

Gallinitas con Vino
Little Chickens with Wine

    5 tablespoons vegetable oil
    1 large onion, sliced
    4 Rock Cornish hens
    2 large tomatoes, peeled and quartered
    ¼ cup chopped parsley
    3 bay leaves
    1 tablespoon vinegar
    ½ teaspoon salt
    ¼ teaspoon pepper
    ½ teaspoon cinnamon
      Dry red wine to cover hens
    1 pickled serrano chili, rinsed, seeded, chopped and drained, optional

Heat the vegetable oil in a Dutch oven. Add onion and the hens; brown hens on all sides. Add remaining ingredients, except serrano chili. Cover and simmer for one hour or until the hens are tender. Remove bay leaves. Place hens in a deep bowl; ladle sauce over. Garnish with chopped serrano chili. Makes 4 servings.

Chicken with Green Chilies

    2 fresh poblano chilies, or bell peppers
    1 3-pound chicken, cut into serving pieces
    ½ teaspoon salt
    4 strips bacon
    1 medium onion, chopped
    4 tablespoons all-purpose flour
    ½ cup chicken bouillon
    1 cup sour cream

Place chilies on a skewer. Roast over a gas flame or broil until the skin is charred and loose. Place peppers in a plastic bag or wrap in a tea towel to steam. Remove skin, seeds and stem; chop. Set aside. Preheat oven to 350°. Place chicken, skin side up, in a roasting pan; sprinkle with salt. Place bacon strips over the chicken and bake for one hour, or until the chicken is tender. Drain three tablespoons drippings from roasting pan. Prepare the sauce. Heat bacon drippings in a small saucepan. Add onion and sauté for two minutes, stirring occasionally. Stir in flour. Add chicken bouillon, stir and simmer until the sauce begins to thicken. Remove from heat. Stir in sour cream. Spoon sauce over chicken. Bake in a 400° oven for ten minutes. Serve with rice, beans and warm tortillas. Makes 4 servings.

Turkey with Green Mole

    1 12-ounce can tomatillos, drained and chopped
    ½ cup pepitas
    ⅓ cup peanuts or almonds
    1 4-ounce can hot or mild green chilies, rinsed, seeded, chopped and drained
    ⅓ cup chopped parsley
    4 tablespoons vegetable oil
  1½ cups chicken broth
    1 10- to 12-pound turkey, roasted and cut into serving pieces

In a blender or food processor, combine tomatillos, pepitas, peanuts, chilies and parsley; puree. Heat oil in a one-quart saucepan. Stir in pureed sauce and broth; heat through. Preheat oven to 350°. Arrange turkey in a baking dish; pour sauce over turkey. Bake for twenty minutes. Serve hot with rice and corn tortillas. Makes 8 to 10 servings.

Roast Turkey with Nogada Sauce

Roast Turkey with Nut Sauce

- 1 6-pound turkey breast
- 3 tablespoons vegetable oil
- ¾ cup ground almonds or walnuts
- 3 tablespoons water
- 2 teaspoons granulated sugar
- ½ cup dry white bread crumbs
- 1 cup light cream
- 1 medium pomegranate, seeded, reserve seeds
- 6 tablespoons chopped parsley

Place turkey breast in a roasting pan. Brush with vegetable oil. Cover loosely with aluminum foil. Roast at 325° for 2 to 2½ hours or until turkey is done. To prepare sauce, combine almonds or walnuts, water, sugar and bread crumbs in a medium-size mixing bowl. Allow ingredients to stand at room temperature for ten minutes. Add cream, mixing well. To serve, slice turkey breast and pour sauce over. Sprinkle pomegranate seeds and parsley on top. Makes 8 servings.

Mole in the Style of Puebla

- 3 dried ancho chilies
- 1 dried chipotle chili
- 1 3½-pound turkey breast, cooked and sliced
- 3 tablespoons sesame seed
- 1 medium onion, chopped
- 1 clove garlic, minced
- 1 corn tortilla, crumbled
- ¾ cup almonds
- ⅛ teaspoon cloves
- ⅛ teaspoon anise
- ¼ teaspoon cinnamon
- ½ cup raisins
- 3 large tomatoes, peeled, seeded and chopped
- 3 tablespoons lard
- 2 cups chicken bouillon
- 1 ounce square unsweetened chocolate
- ½ teaspoon salt

Place peppers in a one-quart saucepan; cover with water. Bring to a boil; reduce heat and simmer for four minutes. Drain chilies; remove seeds, skin and stems. Set aside. Arrange turkey slices in a three-quart casserole or shallow baking dish. Place chilies, sesame seed, onion, garlic, tortilla, almonds, cloves, anise, cinnamon, raisins and tomatoes in a blender or food processor; puree. Heat lard in a two-quart saucepan. Add sauce; simmer for two minutes, stirring constantly. Add bouillon, chocolate and salt; simmer until the chocolate has melted. Sauce should be the thickness of heavy cream. Drizzle sauce over turkey slices. Bake at 325° for twenty minutes. Serve warm with rice and tortillas. Makes 8 servings.

Turkey Enchiladas with Mole Sauce

Filling

- 4 tablespoons lard or vegetable oil
- 1 clove garlic, minced
- 1 large onion, minced
- 4 ribs celery, minced
- 3 cups chopped, cooked turkey

Heat lard or vegetable oil in a ten-inch skillet. Add garlic, onion and celery and sauté for two minutes, or until onion is soft, stirring occasionally. Add turkey, stir and heat through.

Tortillas

- 16 corn tortillas
- 1 cup vegetable oil

Heat oil in an eight-inch skillet. Using tongs to hold tortillas, fry for five seconds on each side. Drain on paper toweling.

Mole Sauce

- 1 clove garlic, minced
- 1 medium onion, minced
- 2 large tomatoes, peeled, seeded and chopped
- 1 tortilla, torn into ½-inch pieces
- ½ cup raisins
- ½ cup peanuts
- ½ teaspoon cinnamon
- ¼ teaspoon ground cumin
- 3 tablespoons vegetable oil
- 1 ounce unsweetened chocolate
- 1½ cups chicken bouillon

Combine all ingredients, except oil, chocolate and bouillon, in a blender or a food processor; puree. Heat oil in a two-quart saucepan. Add sauce and chocolate. Stir in bouillon and simmer for one minute. Sauce should be the consistency of cream. If the sauce is too thick, add more chicken bouillon.

Assemble

- 2 extra large hard-cooked eggs, chopped

Preheat oven to 350°. Dip tortillas in the Sauce. Place three tablespoons Filling in the center of each tortilla. Roll up. Place tortillas, seam side down, in a lightly oiled, 9 x 13-inch casserole. Pour Mole Sauce over enchiladas. Bake for twenty minutes, uncovered. Sprinkle eggs over enchiladas before serving. Makes 8 servings.

Pescado (Fish)

Red Snapper in the Style of Veracruz

- 1 2-pound red snapper, cleaned, scaled, head and tail intact, or 2 pounds fillets
   Juice of ½ lime
- ¼ teaspoon salt
- ¼ teaspoon pepper
- 4 tablespoons vegetable oil
- 2 cloves garlic, minced
- 2 medium onions, sliced
- 3 large tomatoes, peeled and quartered
- ½ cup sliced green olives
- 1 pound new potatoes, boiled, peeled and quartered

Preheat oven to 350°. Coat fish with oil. Place fish in baking dish. Sprinkle lime juice, salt and pepper over fish. Heat oil in a medium-size saucepan. Add garlic and onion and sauté until soft. Stir in tomatoes and olives. Cook for one minute. Pour tomato mixture over fish. Bake for forty-five minutes. Makes 6 servings.

Fish Slices in Citrus Sauce

- ½ cup orange juice
- 4 tablespoons lime juice
- 2 teaspoons lemon juice
- ½ teaspoon salt
- ¼ teaspoon white pepper
- 2½ pounds halibut or any firm fish, washed and drained
- 4 tablespoons vegetable oil
- 2 cloves garlic, minced
- 1 large onion, chopped
- 3 medium tomatoes, peeled, seeded and chopped
- 1 orange, sliced
- 1 lime, sliced

Combine orange, lime and lemon juices, salt and pepper in a small mixing bowl. Cut fish into slices; place in a greased 9x13-inch casserole. Prick fish with a fork. Sprinkle citrus juices over top. Marinate at room temperature for thirty minutes. While fish is marinating, heat oil in a medium-size skillet. Add garlic and onion and sauté over moderate heat until onion is soft, about two minutes. Add tomatoes and cook for one minute, stirring frequently. Spoon vegetables over fish. Bake, uncovered, at 350° for thirty minutes, or until fish is opaque. Place on a serving platter; garnish with orange and lime slices. Makes 4 to 5 servings.

Poached Fish with Shrimp Sauce

- 2½ pounds whitefish, or any firm-fleshed fish, sliced
- 1 large onion, thinly sliced
- 4 bay leaves
- 2 cloves garlic, crushed

Wrap fish in cheesecloth. Fill a five-quart stockpot, two-thirds full of water. Add sliced onion, bay leaves and garlic. Simmer for ten minutes. Add fish; cover. Simmer for thirty minutes, or until the fish flakes easily with a fork. Remove fish; drain. Place a slice of fish on each plate. Spoon on Shrimp Sauce. Makes 6 servings.

Shrimp Sauce

- 4 tablespoons butter
- 2 tablespoons vegetable oil
- 1 large onion, chopped
- 5 tablespoons flour
- 1½ cups milk, cream or half and half
- 2 4½-ounce cans shrimp, washed and drained
- ½ cup chopped cilantro
- ½ teaspoon salt
- ¼ teaspoon white pepper

Heat butter and oil in a ten-inch skillet. Add chopped onion and sauté for two minutes. Stir in flour. Slowly stir in milk; cook for three minutes, stirring constantly. Add remaining ingredients and stir until smooth.

Baked Fish in Bell Pepper Sauce

- 2 pounds firm-fleshed fish, sliced
- ¼ teaspoon salt
- ¼ teaspoon pepper

Sprinkle salt and pepper over fish. Place fish in a 1½-quart casserole. Bake at 350° for twenty minutes. Pour Sauce over fish. Bake until fish is tender, about ten minutes. Makes 4 servings.

Sauce

- 2 tablespoons olive oil
- 2 tablespoons vegetable oil
- ½ teaspoon garlic powder
- 1 large onion, chopped
- 5 large sweet bell peppers, seeded and sliced
- 2 8-ounce cans tomato sauce
- ¼ teaspoon salt

Heat oils in a ten-inch skillet. Add garlic powder, onion and peppers. Sauté for two minutes, stirring occasionally. Stir in tomato sauce and salt. Place pepper mixture in a large mixing bowl. Refrigerate until ready to use.

Codfish and Tomatoes

    2 pounds salted or fresh codfish, soaked 24 hours
      in cold water
    3 tablespoons vegetable oil
    3 tablespoons olive oil
    2 cloves garlic, minced
    2 medium onions, chopped
    1 16-ounce can tomatoes with liquid
    1 16-ounce can sliced potatoes
    ½ teaspoon salt
    ¼ teaspoon white pepper
    1 canned jalapeno pepper, rinsed, drained, seeded
      and chopped
    ½ cup sliced green olives

Drain codfish and cut into one-half inch pieces. Heat oils in a Dutch oven. Add garlic and onion and sauté for two minutes, stirring occasionally. Add codfish and sauté for one minute, stirring occasionally. Add remaining ingredients. Simmer, uncovered, for thirty minutes or until the fish is tender. Makes 4 servings.

Fish with Almond Sauce

    3 tablespoons lime juice
    ½ teaspoon salt
    ½ teaspoon pepper
    2 pounds red snapper fillets
    6 tablespoons butter
    4 tablespoons all-purpose flour
    2 cups half and half
    4 ounces grated Monterey Jack cheese
    ½ cup ground almonds
    ¼ teaspoon nutmeg
    ¼ teaspoon cinnamon
    ⅛ teaspoon cloves

Sprinkle lime juice, salt and pepper over fish. Let stand for thirty minutes at room temperature. Place fish in an oiled two-quart casserole. Preheat oven to 400°. Heat butter in an eight-inch skillet. Stir in flour. Slowly stir in cream and stir until mixture is smooth and begins to thicken. Add remaining ingredients and mix well. Pour sauce over fish. Bake for ten minutes; reduce heat to 350° and bake for fifteen minutes, or until the fish is cooked. Serve with salad and tortillas. Makes 4 servings.

Cook frozen fish while still a little icy in the center. It takes only a few minutes longer to cook, but helps keep the fish moist and juicy.

Shrimp Patties
Patties

    4 extra large eggs, separated
    2 4½-ounce cans shrimp, drained and chopped,
      reserve juice
    ¾ cup cooked Beans, mashed (Recipe on page 43)
    2 tablespoons flour
    ¼ teaspoon salt
    ⅛ teaspoon white pepper
    3 cups vegetable oil

Beat egg whites until stiff; set aside. Beat egg yolks for one minute in a large mixing bowl. Add shrimp, beans, flour, salt and pepper; mix lightly. Fold shrimp mixture into egg whites. Heat oil in a skillet. Slide batter by tablespoonfuls into oil. Fry on both sides until golden brown. Drain on paper toweling. Serve hot with Sauce. Makes 5 to 6 servings.

Sauce

    3 tablespoons vegetable oil
    2 cloves garlic, minced
    1 large onion, chopped
    3 tablespoons all-purpose flour
    4 large tomatoes, peeled and chopped
    ½ teaspoon salt
    ½ teaspoon red pepper flakes

Heat oil in a skillet. Add garlic and onion and sauté for two minutes, stirring occasionally. Stir in flour, until it is absorbed, about one minute. Add tomatoes, salt and pepper flakes; stir for one minute. Place in a covered container and refrigerate until ready to use.

Shrimp with Garlic

    3 tablespoons lime juice
    1½ pounds large shrimp, peeled, deveined,
       leave tail intact
    4 tablespoons butter
    2 tablespoons vegetable oil
    4 cloves garlic, minced
    1 medium onion, chopped
    ¼ teaspoon white pepper

Sprinkle lime juice over shrimp; set aside. Heat butter and oil in a twelve-inch skillet. Add garlic and onion and sauté for two minutes, stirring occasionally. Add shrimp and pepper and sauté until the shrimp turns white, about two minutes, stirring often. Do not overcook shrimp or they will be tough. Serve with rice, beans and tortillas. Makes 5 to 6 servings.

Fish in Adobo Sauce

- 4 dried ancho chilies
- ½ cup orange juice
- 3 large tomatoes, peeled and chopped
- 2 tablespoons vinegar
- ¼ cup chopped cilantro
- 1 medium onion, minced
- ½ teaspoon oregano
- 2 pounds pompano or any firm-fleshed fish
- ½ teaspoon garlic powder
- ¼ teaspoon salt
- 4 tablespoons vegetable oil

Lightly toast ancho chilies in an ungreased skillet. Place in a saucepan, cover with water and cook four minutes. Drain; remove seeds and stem. Combine ancho chilies, orange juice, tomatoes, vinegar, cilantro, onion, oregano, garlic powder and salt in a two-quart saucepan. Simmer for five minutes, stirring occasionally. Set aside. Place fish in a greased casserole. Preheat oven to 350°. Drizzle oil over fish. Cover with sauce. Bake thirty minutes. Makes 4 servings.

Ceviche *Marinated Raw Fish*

- 1 pound sole, cut into ¾-inch pieces
- 2 cups lime juice
- 1 large onion, thinly sliced
- 1 large tomato, peeled, seeded and chopped
- 1 canned jalapeno pepper, rinsed, seeded and chopped
- 3 tablespoons olive oil
- 3 tablespoons vinegar
- ½ teaspoon salt
- ¼ teaspoon pepper

Place sole in a two-quart casserole. Cover with lime juice. Add remaining ingredients; mix gently. Cover with plastic wrap. Refrigerate for two days. Turn fish three times while it is marinating. Serve chilled. Makes 4 to 6 servings.

Fish, Rice and Tomato Sauce

- 6 tablespoons vegetable oil
- 1½ pounds firm-fleshed fish
- 2 cloves garlic, minced
- 1 large onion, chopped
- 1½ cups long-grain rice
- ½ cup hot water
- 2 8-ounce cans tomato sauce

Heat oil in a twelve-inch skillet. Fry the fish on both sides, turning to brown each side. Remove from pan and set aside. Place garlic and onion in skillet and sauté for two minutes, stirring occasionally. Add rice and stir constantly until the rice is coated, about three minutes. Sprinkle water over rice. Stir in tomato sauce. Place fish on top of rice. Reduce heat, cover and simmer for twenty minutes, or until the rice is cooked. Makes 4 servings.

Codfish Fritters

- 2 pounds dried codfish, cut into 2-inch chunks
- ½ teaspoon garlic powder
- 1 medium onion, chopped
- ¼ cup chopped parsley
- 2 cups all-purpose flour
- 2 cups cold water
- 2 teaspoons baking powder
- 3 cups vegetable oil

Place fish in a large mixing bowl. Cover with water and soak for one hour. Drain fish and repeat procedure two more times. Shred the fish and place in a large bowl. Add remaining ingredients, except oil, and mix lightly. Heat the oil to 375° in a ten-inch skillet. Form fish mixture into three-inch patties. Gently slide four patties into the hot oil. Cook until the fish is golden brown on both sides. Turn with a slotted spoon. Drain on paper toweling. Serve immediately. Makes 4 servings.

Fried Fish

- 2 pounds firm-fleshed fish, sliced
- 1 teaspoon salt
- ½ teaspoon pepper
- 1 cup all-purpose flour
- 1 extra large egg, lightly beaten
- ½ cup milk
- 3 cups vegetable oil
- 1 large onion, chopped

Rinse fish and pat dry with paper toweling. Sprinkle salt and pepper over fish. Blend flour, egg and milk in a medium-size mixing bowl. Allow to stand at room temperature for thirty minutes. Heat oil in a ten-inch skillet. Dip fish into batter. Fry six pieces at a time for five minutes, turning to brown both sides. Drain on paper toweling. Serve with chopped onion. Makes 4 servings.

Frijoles y Arroz
(Beans and Rice)

Beans

2 cups dried red, black or pinto beans
6 cups water
2 cloves garlic, crushed
1 large onion, chopped
½ teaspoon basil
1 teaspoon salt
2 tablespoons bacon drippings

Wash beans carefully to remove any foreign particles. Place beans in a heavy four- or five-quart stockpot. Pour water over beans. Add garlic, onion and basil. Simmer, covered, for two hours. Check beans periodically to see if they are still covered with water. If not, add water to cover. Add salt and bacon drippings; mix well. Cover and simmer for one-half hour, or until beans are tender. Serve hot. Makes 6 servings.

Beans with Chorizo *Beans with Sausage*

1 tablespoon bacon drippings
1 medium onion, chopped
1 pound chorizo or Italian sausage
2 medium tomatoes, peeled, seeded and chopped
2 medium green peppers, seeded and chopped
3 cups cooked pinto beans
4 bay leaves

Heat bacon drippings in a heavy twelve-inch skillet. Add onion and sauté until soft, stirring occasionally, about two minutes. Add chorizo and cook over moderate heat about four minutes, stirring frequently. Drain sausage. Remove excess fat from pan. Add remaining ingredients, reduce heat to simmer, and cover. Continue cooking for fifteen minutes, until all ingredients are tender, stirring occasionally. Remove bay leaves. Makes 4 to 5 servings.

Refried Beans

3 strips bacon
2 cups red or pinto beans
6 cups water
2 cloves garlic, crushed
1 large tomato, peeled, seeded and chopped
3 tablespoons bacon drippings
½ teaspoon salt

Fry bacon in a ten-inch skillet. Drain; crumble bacon and reserve drippings. Set bacon aside.

Wash beans carefully to remove any foreign particles. Place beans in a heavy four-quart stockpot. Cover with water. Add garlic and tomato. Cover and simmer for two hours. Stir in bacon drippings and salt. Cover and simmer for one-half hour, or until beans are tender. Drain beans; puree with masher or in a food processor. Return remaining bacon drippings to skillet. Add bacon and beans and fry over moderate heat until beans are quite dry. Taste and correct seasoning. Place beans in a covered container and refrigerate until ready to use. When reheating beans, add water as needed to make beans a pasty consistency. Makes 8 servings.

Chili Bean Tamales

28 fresh or dried corn husks, silk removed
⅓ cup lard or vegetable shortening
1 bouillon cube
1 cup hot water
1½ cups masa harina
¼ teaspoon salt
1 15½-ounce can chili beans, drained and mashed

Trim edges of corn husks two inches from the top and two inches from the bottom; wash. Place husks in a large mixing bowl and cover with hot water. Let stand for one-half hour before using. Beat lard until light and fluffy, in a small mixing bowl. Dissolve bouillon cube in the one cup of hot water. Add masa harina and salt; mix well. Drain husks. Lay two corn husks side by side, one with the wide end up and the other with the wide end down. Overlap edges and seal with masa harina. In center of husks, spread three tablespoons of masa harina to form a 3 x 5-inch rectangle. Top masa harina with two tablespoons of mashed beans. Roll up, jelly-roll fashion; fold one end under and seal with masa harina or tie with string. Leave top side of tamale open. Arrange tamales in a steamer with the open end facing up. Steam for fifty minutes or until the tamales are cooked.* (See page 59.) Carefully uncover steamer. When dough comes away from the husks, the tamales are done. To freeze, wrap in aluminum foil. Makes 14 tamales.

Refried Beans

Refried Bean Enchiladas

Filling

   3 cups Refried Beans (Recipe on page 43)
   ½ cup green olives, chopped
   ½ cup beef stock

Mix all ingredients in a large bowl.

Tortillas

   ½ cup lard or vegetable oil
  12 flour tortillas

Heat oil in a medium-size skillet. Using tongs to hold tortillas, fry for five seconds on each side to soften. Drain on paper toweling.

Sauce

   3 cups Tomato Sauce (Recipe on page 52)

Assemble

   1 cup Guacamole Sauce (Recipe on page 52)

Preheat oven to 350°. Fill each tortilla with three tablespoons Filling. Roll up each tortilla. Place, seam side down, in a shallow, 9 x 13-inch casserole. Spoon Sauce over top. Bake, uncovered, for twenty minutes. Spoon on Guacamole Sauce. Makes 6 servings.

Beans with Beer

   2 cups dried red or pinto beans
   6 cups beer or 3 cups beer plus 3 cups water
   3 tablespoons bacon drippings
   1 medium onion, chopped
   1 15½-ounce can tomatoes, drained and chopped
   ½ teaspoon oregano
   ½ teaspoon salt

Wash beans carefully to remove any foreign particles. Place beans in a heavy four-quart stockpot. Pour beer over beans. Heat bacon drippings in a small skillet. Add onion and sauté until onion is soft. Add onion to beans. Stir in tomatoes and oregano. Cover and simmer for ninety minutes. Stir in salt. If there is not enough liquid, add up to one additional cup beer. Cover and simmer for one hour, or until beans are tender. Serve hot. Makes 6 servings.

Chili Beans

   1 pound pink or pinto beans
   6 cups water
   2 large tomatoes, peeled, seeded and chopped
   ½ teaspoon ground cumin
   2 cloves garlic, crushed
   1 teaspoon salt
   3 tablespoons bacon drippings
   2 teaspoons chili powder

Wash beans carefully to remove any foreign particles. Place beans in a heavy four-quart stockpot. Pour water over beans. Add tomatoes, cumin and garlic. Simmer, covered, for two hours. Add salt, bacon drippings and chili powder; mix lightly. Cover and cook one-half hour or until beans are tender. Makes 6 servings.

Burritos with Refried Beans

   ½ cup Tomato Sauce (Recipe on page 52)
   1 15-ounce can refried beans
   8 10-inch flour tortillas
   2 cups grated Monterey Jack cheese
   2 cups Guacamole (Recipe on page 8)

Heat Tomato Sauce in a medium-size saucepan. Add refried beans and stir constantly for three minutes. Remove from heat; cool to room temperature. Divide filling among the eight tortillas; spread evenly. Sprinkle cheese over refried beans. Fold one inch of bottom and top edges toward the center. Fold sides into the center. Place, seam side down, on a baking sheet. Bake at 350° for ten minutes or until burritos are heated. Garnish with Guacamole. Makes 8 servings.

Refried Beans with Melted Cheese

   3 tablespoons vegetable oil
   1 large onion, chopped
   4 cups pinto beans, cooked and drained
   1 teaspoon chili powder
   ½ teaspoon salt
   ½ pound Monterey Jack cheese, grated

Preheat oven to 350°. Heat oil in a ten-inch skillet. Add onion and sauté until onion is soft, about two minutes, stirring occasionally. Mash beans with a potato masher or use a food processor. Combine beans, chili powder and salt with the onion. Simmer for two minutes; stirring often. Remove beans from heat; place mixture in an oiled 9 x 9-inch baking pan. Sprinkle grated cheese over beans. Bake for twenty minutes, or until cheese is melted. Makes 5 to 6 servings.

Grate cheese onto a wet plate, and it will slip off the plate without sticking.

Frijoles Negros *Black Beans*

2¼ cups black beans
8 cups water
2 tablespoons lard or vegetable oil
1 tablespoon salt
2 sprigs epazote, optional

Wash beans thoroughly, removing any foreign particles. Place beans, water, lard, salt and epazote in a Dutch oven. Bring to a boil. Boil, covered, for two hours, or until beans are tender. Serve with cooking broth. If desired, garnish with sour cream, minced onion or sliced chilies. Makes 6 cups.

White Rice

3 tablespoons lard or vegetable oil
1 cup long-grain rice, washed and drained
2 cups hot water
½ teaspoon salt
¼ teaspoon white pepper

Heat lard or vegetable oil in a one-quart saucepan. Add rice and cook, stirring constantly, until the rice begins to brown. Add the water, salt and pepper; mix lightly. Cover and simmer for twenty minutes. Makes 2 to 3 servings.

Saffron Rice

½ teaspoon saffron
2 tablespoons hot water
1 cup long-grain rice
2 cups water
½ teaspoon salt

Combine saffron and water in a cup; let stand for ten minutes. Strain liquid and pour into a two-quart saucepan. Wash rice and drain. Combine rice, water and salt in the saucepan. Bring rice to a rolling boil; stir and cover. Remove from heat. Let stand for twenty minutes without lifting lid from pan. Makes 2 cups.

Rice with Cheese

2 cups cooked rice
3 large tomatoes, peeled, seeded and chopped
¼ cup raisins
1 large onion, chopped
1 green pepper, seeded and chopped
½ pound Cheddar cheese, grated
1 cup cream-style corn
2 cups bread crumbs

Combine all ingredients, except bread crumbs, in a large mixing bowl. Butter an eight-cup casserole. Place rice mixture in casserole. Top with bread crumbs. Bake for one hour at 350°. Makes 8 servings.

Arroz Mexicano *Mexican Rice*

3 tablespoons lard or vegetable oil
1½ cups long-grain rice, washed and drained
1 clove garlic, minced
1 large onion, chopped
1 large tomato, peeled and chopped
3 cups chicken bouillon

Heat oil in a ten-inch skillet. Add rice and cook, until the rice begins to brown, stirring constantly. Add garlic, onion and tomato; mix well. Sauté for one minute. Stir in bouillon, cover and simmer for twenty minutes. Makes 5 to 6 servings.

Rice with Tomato

4 tablespoons vegetable oil
1 medium onion, chopped
1¼ cups uncooked rice
2 beef bouillon cubes
2 cups hot water
1 large tomato, peeled, seeded and chopped
2 tablespoons chopped parsley
Salt and pepper

Heat oil in a medium-size saucepan. Add onion and sauté until soft, about two minutes, stirring occasionally. Add rice and stir until rice is coated with oil. Combine bouillon with hot water in a small bowl. Add bouillon, tomato, parsley, salt and pepper to taste. Mix well. Cover and simmer for fifteen minutes, stirring once. Cook ten minutes more, or until rice is tender. Makes 4 to 6 servings.

Budin de Arroz

1 quart milk
1 cup uncooked rice, washed and drained
1 cup granulated sugar
4 extra large eggs, lightly beaten
½ teaspoon salt
1 teaspoon vanilla
1 cup raisins
1 teaspoon grated lemon peel
½ teaspoon cinnamon

Place milk and rice in a medium-size saucepan and let stand for one-half hour. Stir rice; cover and simmer for twenty minutes, or until rice is tender. Place rice in a large mixing bowl. Add remaining ingredients and mix thoroughly. Butter an eight-cup soufflé dish. Pour rice pudding into prepared dish. Preheat oven to 375°. Set soufflé dish in a larger pan and add one inch of hot water to the outer pan. Bake for fifty minutes, or until a toothpick inserted in the center comes out clean. Serve warm or chilled. Makes 8 servings.

Huevos y Queso
(Eggs and Cheese)

Scrambled Tortilla Eggs

- 3 tablespoons butter
- 2 corn tortillas
- 8 extra large eggs, lightly beaten
- ½ teaspoon salt
- 1 cup grated Monterey Jack cheese
- 1 large avocado, seeded, peeled and chopped

Melt butter in a twelve-inch skillet. Tear tortillas into bite-size pieces. Add tortilla pieces to butter; fry to soften over low heat for one minute, stirring occasionally. Add eggs; sprinkle with salt. Cook, stirring constantly, until eggs are set. Sprinkle eggs with grated cheese and mix well. Sprinkle avocado pieces over each serving. Makes 4 servings.

Scrambled Eggs

- 2 tablespoons butter
- 1 tablespoon vegetable oil
- 3 green onions, chopped
- 1 red bell pepper, seeded, deveined and sliced lengthwise
- 2 medium tomatoes, peeled, seeded and chopped
- 8 extra large eggs, lightly beaten
- 3 tablespoons milk
- ½ teaspoon salt
- ¼ teaspoon white pepper

Heat butter and oil in a ten or twelve-inch skillet. Add onion and pepper; sauté for two minutes, stirring occasionally. In a large mixing bowl combine remaining ingredients. Pour egg mixture into skillet and scramble until the eggs are set. Serve with black beans and tortillas. Makes 4 servings.

Huevos Rancheros *Ranch Style Eggs*

- ½ cup lard or vegetable oil
- 4 corn tortillas
- 1 clove garlic, minced
- 1 large onion, chopped
- 3 large tomatoes, peeled, seeded and chopped
- 1 4-ounce can mild or hot chili peppers rinsed, seeded and chopped
- ½ teaspoon salt
- 1 tablespoon vegetable oil
- 8 jumbo eggs

Heat the one-half cup oil in a seven-inch skillet. Hold tortilla with tongs or a long fork and fry for five seconds on each side. Drain on paper towel-ing. Place one tortilla on each plate. Remove all but three tablespoons of the lard or oil. Add garlic and onion and sauté until onion is soft. Add tomatoes, peppers and salt. Simmer for about three minutes, until some of the moisture has evaporated, stirring often. Set aside. Heat the one tablespoon oil in a large skillet. Carefully break eggs in skillet. Cook until whites are set. Add one tablespoon water. Cover and cook until eggs are desired degree of doneness. Slip two eggs onto the center of each tortilla. Drizzle hot tomato sauce over each. Serve with Refried Beans (Recipe on page 43). Makes 4 servings.

Eggs and Cheese

- 3 tablespoons bacon drippings
- 1 medium onion, chopped
- 6 extra large eggs, lightly beaten
- 5 tablespoons milk or water
- ¾ cup grated Monterey Jack cheese
- 3 tablespoons chopped parsley

Heat bacon drippings in a medium-size skillet. Add onion and sauté for two minutes, stirring occasionally. In a large mixing bowl, combine eggs, milk and cheese; blend well. Pour egg mixture into heated skillet; cover and cook over low heat until set. Serve on a warm platter, sprinkled with parsley. Makes 3 to 4 servings.

Omelet with Green Chilies

- 3 tablespoons butter
- 1 small onion, chopped
- 3 extra large eggs, lightly beaten
- 4 tablespoons milk
- ¼ teaspoon salt
- ⅛ teaspoon white pepper
- ¼ cup chopped, canned mild or hot green chilies, rinsed and drained
- ½ cup grated sharp Cheddar cheese

Heat butter in an eight-inch skillet. Add onion and sauté for two minutes, stirring occasionally. In a mixing bowl, combine remaining ingredients, except chilies and Cheddar cheese. Add mixture to heated skillet. Cook over low heat until the eggs are set, about four or five minutes. Sprinkle chilies over eggs. Using a spatula, fold the omelet in half. Slide onto a warm serving dish and sprinkle with cheese. Makes 2 servings.

Breakfast Enchiladas

Filling

- 4 tablespoons butter
- 2 medium onions, chopped
- 12 jumbo eggs, lightly beaten

Heat butter in a twelve-inch skillet. Add onion and sauté until onion is soft, about two minutes, stirring occasionally. Add eggs, and cook, stirring constantly until they are set. Remove from heat.

Tortillas

- 12 flour tortillas
- 1 cup vegetable oil

Heat oil in an eight-inch skillet. Using tongs to hold tortillas, fry for five seconds on each side. Drain on paper toweling.

Sauce

- 2 dried ancho chilies
- 3 tablespoons vegetable oil
- 1 medium onion, chopped
- 1 green pepper, seeded and chopped
- 1 16-ounce can whole tomatoes, puree with juice
- 1 8-ounce can tomato sauce
- ½ teaspoon granulated sugar
- ½ teaspoon salt

Place ancho chilies in a one-quart saucepan and cover with water. Simmer for four minutes. Drain; remove skin, seeds and stems. Set aside. Heat oil in a ten-inch skillet. Add onion and pepper and sauté until vegetables are soft, about two minutes, stirring occasionally. Add ancho chilies, tomato puree, tomato sauce, sugar, and salt to the skillet. Simmer for one minute, stirring occasionally.

Assemble

- 2 large avocados, chopped

Preheat oven to 350°. Dip tortillas in Sauce. Place two tablespoons Filling on each tortilla. Roll up. Place tortillas, seam side down, in an oiled 9 x 13-inch casserole. Pour remaining Sauce over enchiladas. Bake, uncovered, for twenty minutes. Top with avocado. Makes 6 servings.

Scrambled Eggs with Tomatillos

- 3 tablespoons vegetable oil
- 1 medium onion, chopped
- ¾ cup (to taste) canned tomatillos, drained, chopped
- 3 tablespoons chopped parsley
- 8 extra large eggs, lightly beaten
- ½ teaspoon salt
- ¼ teaspoon white pepper

Heat oil in a ten-inch skillet. Add onion and sauté for two minutes, stirring occasionally. In a large mixing bowl, combine remaining ingredients; mix well. Pour egg mixture into skillet and scramble until the eggs set. Serve hot with warm tortillas and refried beans. Makes 4 servings.

Chorizo with Eggs

- 2 tablespoons lard or vegetable oil
- ½ pound chorizo
- 1 large onion, chopped
- 8 extra large eggs, lightly beaten
- 5 tablespoons water or milk

Heat lard in a ten-inch skillet. Remove skin from chorizo and crumble sausage into skillet; add onion and sauté until onion is soft and sausage is cooked. Pour off drippings. Combine eggs and water. Add eggs to sausage and scramble until the eggs are set. Serve hot with warm corn tortillas and avocado slices. Makes 4 to 5 servings.

Easy Cheese Enchiladas

Filling

- 3 tablespoons vegetable oil
- 1 large onion, chopped
- 2 cups grated Monterey Jack cheese
- 1 10-ounce can enchilada sauce
- 1 cup sliced black olives

Heat oil in a small skillet. Add onion and sauté over moderate heat for two minutes until soft, stirring occasionally. In a large mixing bowl, combine onion, cheese, enchilada sauce and olives.

Tortillas

- 12 corn tortillas
- ½ cup vegetable oil or lard

Heat oil in a medium-size skillet. Using tongs to hold tortillas, fry for five seconds on each side. Drain on paper toweling.

Sauce

- 2 10-ounce cans enchilada sauce

Assemble

- 1 cup sour cream

Preheat oven to 350°. Fill each tortilla with two tablespoons Filling. Roll tortilla and place, seam side down, in a greased, 9 x 13-inch, casserole. Cover with Sauce. Bake, uncovered, for twenty minutes. Top each enchilada with sour cream. Makes 6 servings.

To separate eggs easily, gently break them into a small funnel over a glass. Yolks will stay in the funnel; the whites flow through.

Huevos con Queso y Jamón

Eggs with Cheese and Ham

- 8 slices American cheese
- 3 slices boiled ham, diced
- ¼ cup chopped sweet pickle
- 8 large eggs
- ½ cup catsup
- 2 tablespoons bottled chili sauce
- 1 tablespoon chili powder (or to taste)
  Salt and pepper to taste
  Pitted ripe olives

Butter an eight-inch baking dish. Place cheese slices in the bottom of dish. Sprinkle on ham and pickles. Carefully break eggs over the top. In a small bowl, combine catsup, chili sauce and chili powder. Spoon mixture over tops of eggs. Dot each egg with a little butter. Salt eggs. Bake in a 300° oven until whites are set and yolks are still soft. Sprinkle with pepper. Garnish with olives. Makes 4 servings.

Fresh Green Chili Peppers with Cheese

- 3 tablespoons butter
- 1 large onion, thinly sliced
- 8 Anaheim chilies
- 1½ cups grated Cheddar cheese
- 1 cup milk
- ½ teaspoon salt
- ¼ teaspoon white pepper

Heat butter in a ten-inch skillet; add onion, and sauté for two minutes. Add chilies and remaining ingredients, mixing well. Simmer until the cheese melts. Serve hot. Makes 4 servings.

Cheese Stuffed Jalapeno Peppers

These peppers are very hot and should only be eaten by the very brave.

- 10 canned, pickled jalapeno peppers
- 5 ounces Cheddar cheese
- ½ cup stuffed olives
- 1 large tomato, cut into eight wedges

Wash and drain peppers. Cut each one lengthwise and remove the seeds. Cut cheese into two-inch slices. Stuff each pepper with cheese. Place on a serving plate, garnish with olives and tomatoes. Cover with plastic wrap and chill until ready to serve. Makes 10 stuffed peppers.

Baked Cheese

A luncheon dish or an appetizer.

- 1 tablespoon butter
- 1¼ pounds Monterey Jack cheese or Cheddar, shredded
- 6 tablespoons chopped onion
- 6 tablespoons chopped pimiento

Preheat oven to 350°. Butter six small baking dishes. Evenly divide the cheese among the dishes. Bake for ten to twelve minutes, until the cheese has melted. Remove from the oven. Sprinkle onions and pimiento over the cheese. Serve hot. Makes 6 servings.

Burritos with Cheese and Chili

- 3 cups grated Monterey Jack cheese
- 8 10-inch flour tortillas
- 2 cups Company Chili (Recipe on page 27)
- 1 large onion, chopped

Divide cheese among the eight tortillas; spread evenly over each tortilla. Fold one inch of bottom and top edges toward the center. Fold sides into the center. Place, seam side down, on a baking sheet. Bake at 350° for ten minutes, or until the burritos are heated through. Place one burrito on each plate. Drizzle chili over each. Sprinkle onion over each burrito. Makes 8 servings.

Cheese Crisps

- 4 large flour tortillas
- 4 tablespoons butter, room temperature
- 8 ounces Monterey Jack cheese, shredded
- 8 ounces Cheddar cheese, shredded

Brush each tortilla with a tablespoon of butter. Preheat oven to 400°. Place tortillas on a baking sheet. Bake for two minutes. Combine cheeses. Sprinkle cheeses over tortillas. Bake for ten minutes, or until cheese has melted. Place on serving dishes and cut into pie-shaped wedges with kitchen shears. Makes 8 servings.

To shred very soft cheese easily, place it in the freezer for fifteen minutes before shredding.

Cheese Tacos with Red Taco Sauce

- 3 tablespoons vegetable oil
- 1 large onion, chopped
- 1 pound Monterey Jack cheese, shredded
- 4 ounces cream cheese, cut into ½-inch cubes
- 8 corn tortillas or taco shells (See page 28)
  Shredded lettuce
  Sour cream
  Red Taco Sauce

Heat oil in a skillet. Add onion and sauté for two minutes, stirring occasionally. Add both cheeses; blend thoroughly. Remove from heat. Fill each taco shell with two tablespoons of the cheese mixture. Serve garnished with lettuce, sour cream and Taco Sauce. Makes 4 servings.

Red Taco Sauce

- 3 tablespoons vegetable oil
- 2 cloves garlic, minced
- 1 13-ounce can tomato sauce
- 6 tablespoons red wine vinegar
- ½ teaspoon salt
- ½ teaspoon red pepper flakes
- ½ cup water

Heat oil in a small saucepan. Add garlic and sauté for thirty seconds. Add remaining ingredients. Simmer for three minutes. Place in a covered container and refrigerate until ready to use.

Melted Cheese and Nopales

- 2 tablespoons butter
- 2 tablespoons vegetable oil
- 1 clove garlic, minced
- 1 large onion, chopped
- 1 19-ounce can nopales or nopalitos, drained
- ½ teaspoon salt
- ¼ teaspoon pepper
- 1 cup grated Monterey Jack cheese

Heat butter and oil in a skillet. Add garlic and onion and sauté for one minute, stirring occasionally. Rinse nopales in cold water three times; drain well. Place nopales in skillet. Simmer for one minute. Add salt, pepper and cheese; mix well. Simmer until the cheese begins to melt. Makes 4 servings.

Cheese Enchiladas
Filling

- 4 tablespoons vegetable oil
- 1 large onion, chopped
- 1 cup sliced black olives
- 2 cups grated Monterey Jack cheese
- 1 8-ounce package cream cheese, cut into ½-inch cubes

Heat oil in a ten-inch skillet. Add onion and sauté for two minutes, or until soft, stirring occasionally. Remove from heat. In a large mixing bowl, combine onion, olives and cheeses.

Tortillas

- 12 corn tortillas
- ½ cup vegetable oil

Heat oil in an eight-inch skillet. Using tongs to hold tortillas, fry for five seconds on each side. Drain on paper toweling.

Sauce

- 2 cups Thick Red Chili Sauce (Recipe on page 52)

Assemble

- 1 cup sour cream

Preheat oven to 350°. Dip each tortilla into sauce. Spoon two tablespoons Filling on each tortilla. Roll up tortillas. Place tortillas, seam side down, in a shallow, 9 x 13-inch casserole. Cover with remaining Sauce. Bake, uncovered for twenty minutes. Top each enchilada with sour cream. Makes 6 servings.

Quesadillas *Filled Turnovers*

- 8 ounces Monterey Jack cheese, grated
- 1 4-ounce can mild chili peppers, rinsed, drained, seeded and chopped
- 1½ cups masa harina
- ½ teaspoon salt
- ¾ cup warm water
- 3 cups vegetable oil or lard

Combine cheese and peppers; set aside. Combine masa harina, salt and warm water, either by hand or in a food processor. Add more water, if necessary. Roll into twelve balls. Press each ball between two sheets of waxed paper to 3½ inches in diameter. Place a tablespoon of filling on one half of the quesadilla. Press the tops over and seal by pinching the edges together. Heat oil to 375° in a large saucepan. Fry three at a time until lightly browned on each side, about two minutes. Serve warm. Makes 12.

Salsas y Rellenos (Sauces and Fillings)

Tomato Sauce

- 7 large tomatoes, peeled, seeded and minced
- 2 cloves garlic, minced
- 4 tablespoons lemon juice
- ¼ teaspoon salt
- ¼ teaspoon pepper
- 6 tablespoons olive oil
- ½ cup chopped parsley

Place tomatoes in a glass bowl. Add garlic, lemon juice, salt and pepper. Add oil in a thin stream, combining with tomatoes as it is poured. Stir in parsley. Place in a covered container and refrigerate until ready to use. Serve with fish or enchiladas. Makes 3½ cups.

Guacamole Sauce

- 2 large avocados, peeled and seeded
- 1 clove garlic, minced
- 1 small onion, minced
- ½ teaspoon salt
- ¼ teaspoon cayenne pepper
- 1 tablespoon olive oil
- 1 tablespoon wine vinegar
- 2 large tomatoes, peeled, seeded and chopped

Mash avocados in a large bowl, blender or food processor. Add garlic, onion, salt, pepper, oil, vinegar and tomatoes. Blend until smooth. Cover with plastic wrap and refrigerate for one hour before serving. Serve with tortilla chips or an assortment of raw vegetables. Makes 2 cups.

Veracruz Sauce

- 3 tablespoons butter
- 2 tablespoons vegetable oil
- 2 cloves garlic, minced
- 2 large onions, chopped
- 4 large tomatoes, peeled, seeded and chopped
- ¼ teaspoon salt
- ⅛ teaspoon black pepper
- ½ cup green olives
- 4 tablespoons capers
- 1 jalapeno pepper, seeded and chopped, optional

Heat butter and oil in a medium-size saucepan. Add garlic and onion and sauté until onion is soft, stirring often. Add tomatoes, salt, pepper, olives, capers and pepper; stir to mix. Simmer for two minutes. Place in a covered container and refrigerate until ready to use. If sauce is too thick when reheated, add water. Makes 3½ cups.

Green Chili Sauce

- 3 tablespoons vegetable oil
- 1 large onion, chopped
- 1 10-ounce can tomatillos, drained and chopped
- ¼ teaspoon salt
- 1 4-ounce can mild green chilies, rinsed, drained and seeded
- 1 cup sour cream

Heat oil in a medium-size saucepan. Add onion and sauté until onion is soft. Add tomatillos, salt and green chilies. Simmer for five minutes, stirring often. Remove from heat; blend in sour cream. Makes 3 cups.

Thick Red Chili Sauce

- 3 tablespoons bacon drippings
- 3 tablespoons all-purpose flour
- 1½ cups chicken bouillon
- ½ cup tomato and jalapeno pepper sauce or ½ cup tomato sauce and ½ teaspoon ground chili
- ½ teaspoon salt
- 2 cloves garlic, minced
- ¼ teaspoon ground cumin
- 1 tablespoon chopped cilantro

Heat bacon drippings in a one-quart saucepan. Add flour and mix well. Slowly add bouillon, a little at a time, stirring constantly. Add remaining ingredients, stirring constantly. Simmer for three to four minutes. Makes 2 cups sauce.

Mole Sauce

- 1 cup chicken stock
- 2 large tomatoes, peeled, seeded and chopped
- 1 ounce unsweetened chocolate, grated
- 2 cloves garlic, minced
- 1 corn tortilla, fried and crumbled
- ⅓ cup peanuts
- ⅓ cup raisins
- 1 tablespoon sesame seed
- ½ teaspoon salt
- ¼ teaspoon cinnamon
- ½ teaspoon chili powder
- 3 tablespoons vegetable oil

Place all ingredients, except oil, in a blender or food processor; puree. Heat oil in a two-quart saucepan. Add puree and heat for thirty seconds, stirring constantly. If sauce is too thick, add more chicken stock. Place in a covered container and refrigerate until ready to use. Makes about 2½ cups sauce.

Hot Green Chili Sauce

- 1 2-ounce can hot green chili peppers
- 1 10-ounce can green tomatoes, drained and chopped
- 2 cloves garlic, minced
- 1 large onion, chopped
- 2 cups beef bouillon
- ¼ teaspoon salt
- 1 4-ounce can mild green chili peppers

Place all ingredients in a three-quart saucepan and simmer for eight minutes, stirring occasionally. Refrigerate in a covered container until ready to use. Makes 3½ cups.

Almond Topping

- 3 tablespoons butter
- 1 tablespoon vegetable oil
- 2 cloves garlic, minced
- 1 small onion, minced
- 1 cup slivered almonds
- 1 cup bread crumbs

Heat butter and oil in an eight-inch skillet. Add garlic and onion and sauté for two minutes, stirring often. Add almonds and bread crumbs; mix well. Sauté for one minute, stirring occasionally. Serve with fish. Makes 2 cups.

Orange Stuffing

- 5 tablespoons butter
- 1 large onion, chopped
- 1 cup chopped celery
- 1 cup sliced mushrooms
- ⅓ cup chopped cilantro
- ½ cup orange juice
- 1 teaspoon grated orange rind
- 5 slices toasted bread, cut into ½-inch cubes

Heat butter in a twelve-inch skillet. Add onion and celery and sauté for two minutes, stirring occasionally. Add mushrooms and sauté for one minute, stirring occasionally. Stir in remaining ingredients; simmer one minute. Good with chicken, turkey or duck. Makes 4 cups.

Potato and Onion Stuffing

- 4 tablespoons butter
- 1 large onion, chopped
- 1 cup chopped celery
- 6 large cooked potatoes, cut into ½-inch cubes
- ½ cup chopped cilantro
- ½ teaspoon salt
- ½ teaspoon Tabasco sauce
- ½ teaspoon ground cumin

Heat butter in a twelve-inch skillet. Add onion and celery and sauté for two minutes, or until soft, stirring occasionally. Add remaining ingredients and simmer for two minutes, stirring occasionally. Place in a covered bowl; refrigerate until ready to use. Serve with turkey or chicken. Makes 6 cups.

Banana Stuffing

- 3 tablespoons butter
- 3 large bananas, sliced
- 1 15½-ounce can tomatoes, drained, seeded and chopped
- 4 tablespoons grated coconut
- 2 tablespoons dark rum, optional

Heat butter in a ten-inch skillet. Add banana slices and sauté, stirring often, for two minutes. Add tomatoes and sauté for three minutes, stirring often. Remove from heat. Stir in coconut and rum. Use to stuff poultry. Makes 4 cups.

Vegetable Stuffing

- 2 tablespoons vegetable oil
- 2 cloves garlic, minced
- 1 large onion, chopped
- 4 large tomatoes, peeled, seeded and chopped
- 6 ribs celery, chopped
- 1 cup sliced mushrooms
- ½ teaspoon oregano
- 1 teaspoon chopped parsley
- ½ teaspoon granulated sugar
- ½ teaspoon salt
- ¼ teaspoon pepper

Heat oil in a ten-inch skillet. Add garlic and onion and sauté until onion is soft, about two minutes, stirring occasionally. Stir in remaining ingredients, simmer for four minutes, stirring occasionally, until most of the moisture has evaporated. Remove from heat; cool. Makes 2 cups.

Turkey Filling

- 1½ cups chopped, cooked turkey
- 1 medium onion, minced
- ⅓ cup Chili Mayonnaise (Recipe on page 17)
- 1 large tomato, peeled, seeded and chopped
- ½ teaspoon salt
- ¼ teaspoon black pepper

Combine all ingredients in a large bowl. Place in a covered container until ready to use; refrigerate. May be served in tomato shells. Makes about 2 cups filling.

Panes (Breads)

Corn Tortillas

- 3 cups masa harina
- ½ teaspoon salt
- 2 tablespoons lard
- 1½ cups water

Combine masa harina, salt and lard in a large mixing bowl. Add water and mix until the masa harina holds its shape and can be formed into a ball. Cover with plastic wrap; let dough rest for twenty minutes. Break into eighteen pieces and roll each into a ball. Place each ball between two pieces of waxed paper and roll out into a 5½- or 6-inch circle, or use a tortilla press. Heat an eight-inch skillet. Do not oil skillet. Peel waxed paper from dough and fry on each side until the tortilla begins to brown, about thirty seconds. Tortillas may be frozen. Makes 18 tortillas.

Flour Tortillas

- 3 cups all-purpose flour
- ½ teaspoon salt
- 1½ teaspoons baking powder
- 2 tablespoons lard
- 1 cup water

Combine flour, salt, baking powder and lard in a large mixing bowl. Add water and mix until the dough holds its shape and can be formed into a ball. Cover with plastic wrap, and let dough rest for twenty minutes. Turn dough out onto a lightly floured board. Roll into a rope. Divide into eighteen pieces. Roll each piece into a ball. Roll each ball into a six-inch circle, or use a tortilla press. Heat an eight-inch skillet. Do *not* oil skillet. Holding tortilla with tongs, fry on each side until it begins to brown, about thirty seconds. Makes 18 to 20 tortillas.

Panes de Oaxaca

- 1 cup warm water
- 1 tablespoon shortening
- 1 teaspoon salt
- 1 teaspoon granulated sugar
- 2 teaspoons baking powder
- 1 teaspoon baking soda
- 2 to 3 cups flour

Place warm water and shortening in a mixing bowl. Let stand until shortening melts. Stir in salt, sugar, baking powder and baking soda. Add one cup flour and mix well. Gradually add remaining flour until dough is too thick to stir. Turn dough out onto a floured surface and knead for fifteen to twenty minutes. Shape dough into a ball. Push fingers through center and pull apart to make a large doughnut shape. Place dough in a well greased casserole. Make six slashes in the top of the dough. Bake in a 350° oven for fifty minutes, or until golden brown. Makes 1 loaf.

How to Use a Tortilla Press

Place waxed paper or a plastic bag on the tortilla press. Place a ball of dough slightly off center and toward the back hinge. Place waxed paper or a sandwich bag on top.

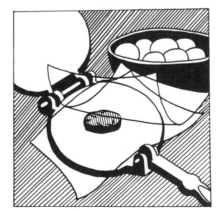

Lower the lid and press firmly to make a five- to six-inch circle.

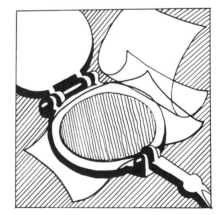

Raise lid; remove waxed paper from top. Peel off waxed paper from bottom. Fry in heated skillet as directed in recipes above.

Pan Dulce *Streusel Sweet Bun*
Concha *Shell*

4 tablespoons butter
1 cup milk
1 package active dry yeast
¼ cup warm water (105° to 115°)
½ cup granulated sugar
4½ to 5 cups all-purpose flour
½ teaspoon salt
2 extra large eggs

Heat butter and milk in a one-quart saucepan over moderate heat until butter has melted. Remove from heat and cool to room temperature. Combine yeast and warm water in a cup. Stir to dissolve yeast. Let stand five minutes in a draft-free area. Combine sugar, flour, salt and eggs in a large mixing bowl. Add yeast and milk mixture to flour and mix well. Turn out onto a lightly floured board and knead for five minutes, or until smooth and elastic. Place dough in a greased bowl; turn dough to grease the top. Cover with oiled aluminum foil. Let rise in a draft-free area for one hour or until doubled in bulk. When dough has doubled, punch down and turn out onto a lightly floured board and knead for one minute. Tear dough in half; roll each half into a rope. Break each rope into seven pieces. Butter two baking sheets. On a lightly floured surface, pat each ball into a three-inch round. Sprinkle three tablespoons of Streusel over each dough round. Score each round with a sharp knife in four semicircle lines resembling a shell. Place on the prepared baking sheets. Cover with oiled aluminum foil and place in a draft-free area. Let rise until doubled in bulk, about forty-five minutes. Preheat oven to 375°. Brush tops of Concha with Egg Wash. Bake twenty to twenty-five minutes. Cool. Makes 14 rolls.

Streusel

1½ cups granulated sugar
2 cups all-purpose flour
1½ sticks butter at room temperature
6 extra large egg yolks

Combine all ingredients in a large bowl. Cover with plastic wrap and refrigerate until needed.

Egg Wash

1 extra large egg, lightly beaten
1 tablespoon milk

Combine eggs and milk in a cup. Mix lightly.

Pumpkin Muffins

1 cup granulated sugar
4 tablespoons butter, at room temperature
2 extra large eggs
1¼ cups pumpkin
1 cup milk
1½ cups all-purpose flour
2 teaspoons baking powder
1 teaspoon cinnamon
¼ teaspoon cloves
¼ teaspoon allspice
¼ teaspoon salt
½ cup raisins
4 tablespoons granulated sugar
½ teaspoon cinnamon

Preheat oven to 400°. Cream the butter and the one cup sugar. Add eggs and pumpkin and mix well. Blend in milk. Combine flour, baking powder, the one teaspoon cinnamon, cloves, allspice and salt. Gradually beat into pumpkin mixture, beating well after each addition. Fold in raisins. Butter muffin tins. Fill two-thirds full with batter. Combine the four tablespoons sugar and one-half teaspoon cinnamon. Sprinkle over batter. Bake for twenty minutes or until muffins are golden. Makes 18.

Spoon Bread

1 17-ounce can cream-style corn
1 cup yellow cornmeal
⅓ cup bacon drippings or lard or vegetable shortening
2 extra large eggs, lightly beaten
1 teaspoon baking soda
1 4-ounce can mild green peppers, rinsed, drained, seeded and chopped
1 cup grated Monterey Jack cheese

Butter a 9 x 9-inch baking pan. Preheat oven to 400°. Combine all ingredients, except cheese, in a large mixing bowl. Pour into prepared pan. Sprinkle cheese over top of bread. Bake forty minutes, or until golden brown. Cool. Makes 9 pieces.

Cheese Bread

3 tablespoons butter
1 cup milk
½ cup grated Colby cheese
⅓ cup chopped pimiento
1 package active yeast
1 tablespoon water
¼ cup water (105° to 115°)
2½ to 3 cups all-purpose flour

Place butter and milk in a one-quart saucepan over medium heat until butter melts. Remove from heat; add cheese and pimiento and stir until the cheese melts. Combine yeast, sugar and water in a cup; stir to dissolve yeast. Let stand in a draft-free area for five minutes. Combine flour, yeast and milk mixture in a large mixing bowl; mix well. Turn dough out onto a lightly floured board and knead until dough is smooth and elastic. Place dough in an oiled bowl; cover with oiled aluminum foil. Let rise in a draft-free area for about one hour or until doubled in bulk. Punch dough down, place onto lightly floured board, knead for thirty seconds. Butter a 9 x 5 x 3-inch loaf pan. Place dough in prepared loaf pan. Cover with oiled aluminum foil; place in a draft-free area for about one hour, or until it has doubled in bulk. Preheat oven to 375°. Bake for thirty to thirty-five minutes. Turn out of pan and cool on a

Three Kings Bread

⅓ cup warm water (105° to 115°)
1 package active dry yeast
1 teaspoon granulated sugar
2 cups all-purpose flour
½ cup granulated sugar
6 tablespoons butter, melted and cooled to room temperature
¼ teaspoon salt
2 extra large eggs, lightly beaten
¾ cup raisins, washed and drained
½ cup all-purpose flour
3 tablespoons butter, melted
1 cup confectioners' sugar, sifted
5 tablespoons milk
1 tablespoon lemon juice
8 red cherries
8 green cherries
¼ cup blanched, sliced almonds

Combine warm water, yeast and one teaspoon sugar in a cup. Stir to dissolve yeast. Let stand five minutes in a draft-free area. Combine flour, sugar, butter, salt and eggs in a large mixing bowl. Coat raisins with one-half cup flour in a small mixing bowl. Add to dough mixture. Turn out onto a lightly floured board. Knead until dough is smooth and elastic. Place in a greased bowl; turn dough to grease the top. Let stand loosely covered with buttered aluminum foil in a warm place for one hour or until doubled in bulk. Turn dough onto a lightly floured board. Knead until smooth and elastic. Shape into a circle on a

buttered baking sheet. Make one-inch cuts around the outside with a pair of kitchen scissors. Cover loosely with buttered aluminum foil. Place in a draft-free area for one hour or until doubled in bulk. Preheat oven to 350°. Brush bread with melted butter. Bake for thirty minutes. Combine confectioners' sugar, milk and lemon juice. Drizzle icing over bread while it is still warm. Decorate with cherries and almonds. Makes 1 loaf.

Sopaipillas *Puffy Fried Bread*

2 cups all-purpose flour
¼ teaspoon salt
1½ tablespoons baking powder
4 tablespoons vegetable shortening
⅔ cup water
3 cups vegetable oil
½ cup granulated sugar

Combine flour, salt, baking powder and shortening and mix until shortening is blended. Add water and mix well. Turn out onto a lightly floured board. Knead until smooth, about two minutes. Roll into a ball. Cover and refrigerate for twenty minutes. Cut dough in half. Roll out one ball on a lightly floured board, into a twelve-inch square. Cut into three-inch squares. Roll out remaining dough and cut into squares. Heat oil to 375° in an eight-inch skillet. Fry sopaipillas, two at a time, for twenty-five seconds on each side, or until golden brown. Remove with a slotted spoon. Drain on paper toweling. Sprinkle sugar on top. Serve warm or cool. Makes 32.

Banana Nut Bread

½ cup butter at room temperature
½ cup granulated sugar
½ cup firmly packed light brown sugar
2 extra large eggs
3 medium bananas, mashed
2 cups flour
1 teaspoon baking powder
1 teaspoon baking soda
¼ teaspoon salt
½ cup milk
1 cup chopped almonds

Preheat oven to 350°. Butter a 9 x 5-inch loaf pan. Cream butter and sugars. Add eggs and mix lightly. Add bananas and mix well. Sift together flour, baking powder, baking soda and salt. Add to butter mixture and mix well. Add milk and mix well. Stir in almonds. Pour into prepared pan. Bake for fifty to sixty minutes, or until bread tests done. Cool on cake rack. Makes 1 loaf.

Sweet Tamales

- 28 fresh or dried corn husks, silk removed
- ⅓ cup vegetable shortening
- 1½ cups masa harina
- ¼ teaspoon salt
- ¾ cup warm water
- 1 cup chopped walnuts
- 3 tablespoons orange rind
- 3 tablespoons orange juice
- 6 tablespoons brown sugar

Trim edges of corn husks, two inches from the top and two inches from the bottom; wash. Place husks in a large mixing bowl and cover with hot water; let stand for one-half hour before using. Place shortening in a small mixing bowl and beat until light and fluffy. Combine masa harina, salt and warm water in medium-size mixing bowl. Add shortening and mix until smooth. Drain husks. Lay two cornhusks side by side, one with the wide end up and the other with the wide end down. Overlap edges and seal with masa harina. In center of husks, spread three tablespoons of masa harina to form a 3 x 5-inch rectangle. Combine walnuts, orange rind, orange juice and brown sugar in small mixing bowl. Top masa harina with two tablespoons of filling. Roll up, jelly-roll fashion; fold one end under and seal with masa harina or tie with string. Arrange in a steamer* with the open ends facing up. Steam for fifty minutes or until tamales are cooked. Carefully uncover steamer. When the dough comes away from the husks, the tamales should be done. Tamales can be frozen if wrapped in aluminum foil. Thaw before reheating. Reheat in a 350° oven. Makes 14 tamales.

*If you do not have a steamer, invert a heatproof soup bowl in a Dutch oven and place a dinner plate over the soup bowl. Pour water under the plate.

Borracho Cake *Rum Flavored Sponge Cake*

- 4 jumbo eggs, separated
- ½ cup cake flour
- ½ cup granulated sugar
- ¼ teaspoon salt

Preheat oven to 350°. Place egg whites in a small bowl and beat until stiff peaks form. Sprinkle flour over egg whites; gently fold into egg whites. Beat egg yolks until lemon colored. Add sugar and salt; mix lightly. Fold egg yolks into egg whites. Pour batter into a lightly buttered nine-inch springform. Bake for forty minutes. Prepare Syrup. Remove cake from oven and cool for five minutes. Place on a serving plate. Prick top of cake with a toothpick. Ladle Syrup over cake. Cake will absorb Syrup. Makes 8 servings.

Syrup

- 1 cup granulated sugar
- ¾ cup water
- 1 3-inch cinnamon stick
- ⅓ cup light rum

Place sugar, water and cinnamon stick in a one-quart saucepan and bring to a boil. Reduce heat and simmer for three minutes. Remove cinnamon stick. Add rum and mix well. Cool.

Capirotada *Holiday Cheese Pudding*

- ¼ pound butter, melted
- 12 slices toasted bread
- 8 ounces Longhorn cheese, shredded
- 2 tablespoons chopped parsley
- 2 apples, peeled and sliced
- 1 cup raisins
- 1½ cups firmly packed dark brown sugar
- 2 cups hot water
- ¾ teaspoon cinnamon

Dip each slice of toast in melted butter. Layer six slices of the toast in an eight-cup casserole. Sprinkle cheese over toast. Combine parsley, apple and raisins in a small mixing bowl. Arrange parsley mixture over cheese. Dip remaining toast in butter. Place toast over parsley mixture. Place brown sugar, hot water and cinnamon in a two-quart saucepan; bring to a boil and boil for one minute. Pour over toast. Bake at 375° for twenty-five minutes. Serve warm. Makes 6 to 8 servings.

Dulce de Mango *Mango Dessert*

- 1 cup water
- 1¾ cups granulated sugar
-   Juice of 1 lemon
- 6 large, ripe mangoes, peeled and sliced

Place water, sugar and lemon juice in a large saucepan. Simmer for thirty minutes. Add mangoes and simmer until syrup is reduced to about half. Remove from heat and chill before serving. Makes 6 servings.

Sweet Empanadas *Sweet Potato Turnovers*
Pastry

- 2 cups all-purpose flour
- ¼ teaspoon salt
- 4 tablespoons lard, cut into ½-inch pieces
- 3 tablespoons butter, cut into ½-inch pieces
- 6 to 7 tablespoons ice water
- 1 egg, lightly beaten
  Confectioners' sugar

Combine flour, salt, lard, and butter in a mixing bowl. Cut in lard and butter with a pastry cutter. Add ice water one tablespoon at a time; mix until a soft ball is formed. Cover dough with plastic wrap; refrigerate for two hours. Preheat oven to 375°. Roll out dough on a lightly floured surface to one-eighth inch thickness. Cut circles with a three-inch cookie cutter. Place two teaspoons Filling in the center of each circle. Brush edges with beaten egg. Fold in half. Twist to seal. Place empanadas on a buttered baking sheet. Brush egg over tops of empanadas. Bake twenty-five minutes or until golden brown. Remove from baking sheet and sprinkle with confectioners' sugar. Cool. Makes 17 empanadas.

Filling

- 4 small sweet potatoes, peeled and boiled or
  1 17-ounce can yams, drained
- ½ cup firmly packed dark brown sugar
- ½ cup raisins
- ¼ teaspoon salt

Mash sweet potatoes in a mixing bowl with masher or use a food processor. Add brown sugar, raisins and salt. Mix thoroughly.

Rosette Cookies

- 1 cup all-purpose flour
- 1 cup milk
- ¼ teaspoon salt
- 2 tablespoons granulated sugar
- 1 extra large egg
- 4 drops red food coloring, optional
- 3 cups vegetable oil
- ½ cup granulated sugar
- 1 tablespoon cinnamon

Combine all ingredients, except the oil, one-half cup sugar and the cinnamon, in a large mixing bowl. Let stand for twenty minutes; stir. Heat oil to 375° in a ten-inch skillet. Dip mold into oil for twenty seconds; drain on paper toweling. Dip mold halfway into the batter. Place mold in oil for eight seconds or until cookie is golden brown. Remove cookie from the mold by prodding with a knife. Remove cookie from oil with a fork or a slotted spoon. Drain on paper toweling. Fry two cookies at a time until all batter has been used. Combine sugar and cinnamon in a small bowl. Sprinkle sugar mixture over cookies. Store cooled cookies in an airtight container. Makes 5 dozen.

Churros *Crullers*

- 1 cup water
- 1 cup all-purpose flour
- 3 tablespoons granulated sugar
- ¼ teaspoon salt
- 2 extra large eggs
- 1 teaspoon sherry
  Oil for deep frying
- ½ cup granulated sugar

Bring water to a boil in a 1½-quart saucepan. Remove from heat. Add flour, sugar and salt. Beat vigorously until batter is fluffy and smooth. Add eggs, one at a time, beating well after each addition. Add sherry and continue beating until batter is smooth. Heat oil to 375° in a ten-inch skillet. Using a pastry bag fitted with a star tip, carefully squeeze three-inch strips of batter into hot oil. Fry about fifteen seconds, turning to brown on all sides. Drain on paper toweling. Roll each cruller in sugar while hot. Makes 12 crullers.

Almond Pralines

- 1 cup firmly packed dark brown sugar
- 1 cup granulated sugar
- 1 cup light cream
- 2 tablespoons butter, cut into chunks
- ½ pound blanched almonds
- 1 teaspoon vanilla

Line two baking sheets with waxed paper or buttered aluminum foil. Combine brown sugar, granulated sugar and cream in a heavy three-quart saucepan. Simmer until the sugar is dissolved, stirring occasionally. Increase heat and bring to a boil. Reduce heat and continue cooking, without stirring, until mixture registers soft-ball stage on a candy thermometer, about fifteen to twenty minutes. Remove saucepan from heat. Add butter. Mix with a wooden spoon until the mixture begins to thicken, about five minutes. Add almonds and vanilla. Drop by tablespoonfuls onto waxed paper. Let stand until completely cooled. Wrap individually in waxed paper. Store in a cool, dry area. Makes 20.

Fried Bananas

1¼ cups all-purpose flour
1 jumbo egg
1 cup milk
¼ teaspoon salt
8 large bananas, peeled and cut in half lengthwise, then cut into 3-inch pieces
¼ cup light rum
½ cup granulated sugar
¾ teaspoon cinnamon
2 cups vegetable oil
½ cup confectioners' sugar

Combine flour, egg, milk and salt in a medium-size mixing bowl; let batter stand for twenty minutes. Place bananas in a glass dish; pour rum over all. Combine sugar and cinnamon and sprinkle over bananas. Heat oil to 380° in a large skillet. Dip bananas in batter. Fry six at a time, turning to brown both sides. Remove with a slotted spoon. Drain on paper toweling. Sprinkle bananas with confectioners' sugar. Serve hot. Makes 4 to 5 servings.

Banana Cream Pie

Pastry

1 9-inch pie crust, baked

Filling

1 cup milk
½ cup granulated sugar
¼ cup milk
5 tablespoons cornstarch
3 extra large egg yolks, lightly beaten
2 large bananas, sliced

Combine the one cup milk and sugar in a one-quart saucepan. Warm mixture over medium heat. Combine the remaining milk and the cornstarch, mixing well to blend. Add cornstarch mixture and egg yolks to saucepan; mix well. Simmer over low heat, stirring constantly, until the mixture thickens. Remove from heat; cool. Arrange bananas on the bottom of the pie crust. Stir filling twice while cooling. Pour into pie shell. Refrigerate for three hours. Prepare Meringue.

Meringue

3 egg whites, room temperature
¼ teaspoon cream of tartar
4 tablespoons sugar

Preheat oven to 425°. Beat egg whites until soft peaks form. Sprinkle cream of tartar and sugar over egg whites. Beat until stiff peaks form. Mound meringue over chilled pie. Bake pie for five minutes, until the top of the meringue is lightly browned. Serve immediately. Makes 6 servings.

Individual Flans

4 tablespoons brown sugar
2 jumbo eggs, lightly beaten
1 cup evaporated milk
⅔ cup water
⅓ cup granulated sugar
1½ teaspoons vanilla
¼ teaspoon salt

Preheat oven to 350°. Lightly press one tablespoon brown sugar into each of four custard cups. Combine remaining ingredients in a large bowl and mix well. Pour carefully into custard cups. Set cups into a shallow pan; add one inch of water to pan. Bake fifty minutes or until set. (A knife inserted into the custard will come out clean.) Loosen edges with a spatula and unmold on individual serving plates. Makes 4 servings.

Party Flan

Caramel

½ cup granulated sugar
2 tablespoons water

Place sugar and water in a small saucepan. Cook over moderate heat, stirring until sugar melts and forms a light brown syrup. Pour syrup into a six-cup mold; tip from side to side to coat the pan; refrigerate until needed.

Custard

6 jumbo eggs
½ cup granulated sugar
¼ teaspoon salt
1 teaspoon vanilla
3½ cups milk

Preheat oven to 350°. Fill a pan that is larger than the mold with 1½ inches of water. Place in oven. Combine eggs, sugar and salt in a large mixing bowl; beat until thick and lemon-colored. Mix vanilla and milk together; slowly add to egg mixture and mix well. Pour into prepared mold. Place mold in the pan in the oven. Bake fifty to sixty minutes, or until flan has set. Chill one hour. Loosen edges with spatula; unmold on serving plate. Makes 8 servings.

Acapulco Pineapple Custard

Sauce

      2 cups cocoa
      2 cups granulated sugar
   1½ cups hot water
   ⅛ teaspoon salt
      1 teaspoon vanilla

Place all ingredients in a 1½-quart saucepan. Boil for three minutes, stirring occasionally. Pour into a container, cover and refrigerate until ready to use.

Custard

      2 13-ounce cans evaporated milk
   ¾ cup granulated sugar
      4 extra large eggs, lightly beaten
   ½ teaspoon cinnamon
      1 8½-ounce can chunk pineapple, undrained

Lightly oil a six-cup ring mold. Preheat oven to 375°. Combine evaporated milk, sugar, eggs, cinnamon, pineapple and juice in a large mixing bowl. Pour into prepared ring mold. Place mold in a large pan. Pour hot water around the mold to a depth of one inch from the top of the mold. Bake, uncovered, for sixty minutes or until a blade inserted into the custard comes out clean. Chill before unmolding. To unmold, run a sharp knife around the edge of the custard. Place a serving plate over the mold and invert carefully. Pour chocolate sauce into a serving bowl. To serve, cut custard carefully with a pie knife and drizzle on sauce with a spoon. Makes 8 servings.

Huevos Reales *Royal Eggs*

   10 extra large egg yolks
      3 tablespoons raisins
      5 tablespoons white rum
   1¾ cups granulated sugar
      1 2-inch cinnamon stick *or* ½ teaspoon
         ground cinnamon
   ⅛ teaspoon nutmeg
   ¾ cup water
   ½ cup crumbled walnuts or toasted
         almonds, optional

Butter a 9 x 9 x 2-inch baking dish. Preheat oven to 350°. Beat egg yolks until lemon colored; pour into baking dish. Place the baking dish into a larger pan and place in the oven; fill the larger pan with one-inch hot water. Bake twenty-five minutes or until eggs are set; cool. While the eggs are cooling, prepare the sauce. Combine raisins and rum; let stand for fifteen minutes. In a small saucepan, combine sugar, cinnamon stick, nutmeg and water. Bring to a boil over medium heat; stir and cook for four minutes, or until the sugar has dissolved. Add raisins and rum. Cut eggs into small squares or triangles; loosen edges and remove to a serving dish. Pour sauce over eggs; chill for at least one hour. Sprinkle nuts over eggs and serve. Makes 6 to 8 servings.

Cocoa Meringues

      4 extra large egg whites at room temperature
   ⅛ teaspoon salt
   ¼ teaspoon cream of tartar
      2 cups granulated sugar
      1 teaspoon vanilla
      2 tablespoons cocoa

Place egg whites in a large mixing bowl and beat until soft peaks form. Sprinkle salt and cream of tartar over egg whites. Continue beating the egg whites, gradually adding sugar, two tablespoons at a time until all sugar is absorbed and stiff peaks are formed. Add vanilla and sprinkle cocoa over the egg whites; mix thoroughly. Cover a baking sheet with parchment paper, waxed paper or aluminum foil. Preheat oven to 275°. Drop batter by teaspoonfuls onto prepared baking sheet. Bake for two hours or until cookies are dry. Makes 26 cookies.

Bunuelos *Fried Cookies*

   ½ cup milk
   2½ cups all-purpose flour
      4 tablespoons melted butter
   ¼ teaspoon salt
   ¾ teaspoon baking powder
      1 extra large egg
      3 cups vegetable oil
   ½ cup granulated sugar
      1 teaspoon cinnamon

Combine milk, flour, butter, salt, baking powder and egg in a large mixing bowl. Place dough on lightly floured board and knead for two minutes or until smooth. Divide dough into twenty-four balls; place on a baking sheet. Refrigerate for twenty minutes. Roll each ball on a lightly floured board to a three-inch diameter. Heat oil to 375° in a seven-inch skillet. Fry cookies one at a time, for twenty seconds on each side, or until golden brown. Remove with slotted spoon and drain on paper toweling. Combine sugar and cinnamon. Sprinkle sugar mixture over cookies. Makes 24 Bunuelos.

Index